Rio de Janeiro

Alex & Gardênia Robinson

Credits

Footprint credits
Editor: Nicola Gibbs
Production and layout: Emma Bryers
Maps: Kevin Feeney

Publisher: Patrick Dawson
Managing Editor: Felicity Laughton
Advertising: Elizabeth Taylor
Sales and marketing: Kirsty Holmes

Photography credits
Front cover: Alex Robinson
Back cover: Alex Robinson

Printed in Great Britain by Alphaset,
Surbiton, Surrey

Every effort has been made to ensure
that the facts in this guidebook are
accurate. However, travellers should
still obtain advice from consulates,
airlines, etc, about travel and visa
requirements before travelling. The
authors and publishers cannot accept
responsibility for any loss, injury or
inconvenience however caused.

The content of Footprint *Focus
Rio de Janeiro* has been taken directly
from Footprint's *Brazil Handbook*,
which was researched and written
by Alex and Gardênia Robinson.

Publishing information
Footprint *Focus Rio de Janeiro*
2nd edition
© Footprint Handbooks Ltd
February 2014

ISBN: 978 1 909268 88 3
CIP DATA: A catalogue record
for this book is available from
the British Library

® Footprint Handbooks and the
Footprint mark are a registered
trademark of Footprint Handbooks Ltd

Published by Footprint
6 Riverside Court
Lower Bristol Road
Bath BA2 3DZ, UK
T +44 (0)1225 469141
F +44 (0)1225 469461
footprinttravelguides.com

Distributed in the USA by Globe
Pequot Press, Guilford, Connecticut

Contents

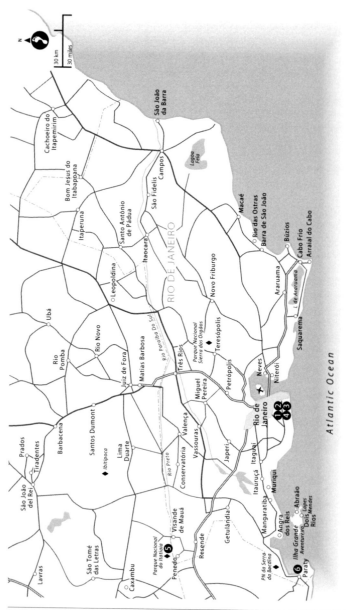

Even those who know nothing else of Brazil will have heard of Rio, its Mardi Gras carnival and its spectacular beach and mountain scenery. What many do not realize is that Rio de Janeiro is a state as well as a city, and that this state boasts beaches, forests and mountains just as beautiful as those in its capital. The southern coast, or Costa Verde, is fringed with emerald-green coves and bays that rise steeply to rainforest-covered hills pocked with national parks. Mountains swathed in coffee plantations sit behind Rio itself, with hill retreats once favoured by the imperial family dotted throughout their valleys and remnants of one of the world's most biodiverse forests covering parts of their slopes. To the northeast of the city lies a string of surf beaches and little resorts, the most celebrated of which is Búzios, a fishing village put on the map by Brigitte Bardot in the late 1960s, which has grown to become a chic little retreat for the state's middle classes.

Planning your trip

Best time to visit Rio de Janeiro

The best time to visit Rio is from April to June, and August to October. Business visitors should avoid mid-December to the end of February, when it is hot and people are on holiday. In these months, hotels, beaches and transport tend to be very crowded. July is a school holiday month. Be aware that some tourist sights may be closed in low season.

Rio has one of the healthiest climates in the tropics, with trade winds keeping the air fresh. July and August are the coolest months, with temperatures ranging from 22°C (18°C in a cold spell) to 32°C on a sunny day at noon. December to March is hot and humid, with temperatures of 32-42°C. October to March is the rainy season; the annual rainfall is about 1120 mm.

Carnaval is a movable feast, running for five riotous days from the Friday afternoon before Shrove Tuesday to the morning hangover of Ash Wednesday. For Carnaval dates, see page 86.

Getting to Rio de Janeiro

Air

Flights into Brazil usually arrive at **Cumbica International Airport** at Guarulhos (which is often used as an alternative name) in São Paulo, or **Tom Jobim International Airport** (also known as Galeão) on the Ilha do Governador, 16 km from the centre of Rio de Janeiro (see page 23). There is a shuttle flight between the two. Airports at Brasília, Salvador, Belo Horizonte, Fortaleza, Manaus and Recife also have connections with the USA and Europe.

Prices are cheapest in October, November and after Carnaval and at their highest in the European summer and the Brazilian high seasons (generally 15 December to 15 January, the Thursday before Carnaval to the Saturday after Carnaval, and 15 June to 15 August). Departure tax is usually included in the cost of the ticket.

Air passes

TAM and GOL offer a 21-day **Brazil Airpass**, which is valid on any TAM destination within Brazil. The price varies according to the number of flights taken and the international airline used to arrive in Brazil. They can only be bought outside Brazil. Rates vary depending on the season. Children pay a discounted rate; those under three pay 10% of the adult rate. Some of the carriers operate a blackout period between 15 December and 15 January.

Don't miss...

Numbers related to the map on page 4.

Baggage allowance

Airlines will only allow a certain weight of luggage without a surcharge; for Brazil this is usually two items of 32 kg but may be as low as 20 kg; with two items of hand luggage weighing up to 10 kg in total. UK airport staff can refuse to load bags weighing more than 30 kg. Baggage allowances are higher in business and first class. Weight limits for internal flights are often lower, usually 20 kg. In all cases it is best to enquire beforehand.

Transport in Rio de Janeiro

Public transport in Brazil is very efficient, but distances are huge. Most visitors will find themselves travelling by buses and planes. Train routes are practically non-existent, car hire is expensive and hitchhiking not advisable. Taxis vary widely in quality and price but are easy to come by and safe when taken from a *posto de taxis* (taxi rank).

Air

Because of the size of the country, flying is often the most practical option and internal air services are highly developed. All state capitals and larger cities are linked with each other with services several times a day, and all national airlines offer excellent service. Recent deregulation of the airlines has greatly reduced prices on some routes and low-cost airlines offer fares that can often be as cheap as travelling by bus (when booked through the internet). Paying with an international credit card is not always possible online; but it is usually possible to buy an online ticket through a hotel, agency or willing friend without surcharge. Many of the smaller airlines go in and out of business sporadically. **Avianca** ⓘ *www.avianca.com.br*, **Azul** ⓘ *www.voeazul.com.br*, **GOL** ⓘ *www.voegol.com.br*, **TAM** ⓘ *www.tam.com.br*, and **TRIP** ⓘ *www.voetrip.com.br*, operate the most extensive routes.

Road

The best paved highways are heavily concentrated in the southeast, but roads serving the interior are being improved to all-weather status and many are paved. Most main roads between principal cities are paved. Some are narrow and therefore dangerous; many are in poor condition.

Bus There are three standards of bus: *Comum*, or *Convencional*, are quite slow, not very comfortable and fill up quickly; *Executivo* are more expensive, comfortable (many have reclining seats), and don't stop en route to pick up passengers so are safer; *leito* (literally 'bed') run at night between the main centres, offering reclining seats with leg rests, toilets, and sometimes refreshments, at double the normal fare. For journeys over 100 km, most buses have chemical toilets (bring toilet paper). Air conditioning can make buses cold at night, so take a jumper; on some services blankets are supplied.

Buses stop fairly frequently (every two to four hours) at *postos* for snacks. Bus stations for interstate services and other long-distance routes are called *rodoviárias*. They are frequently outside the city centres and offer snack bars, lavatories, left luggage, local bus services and information centres. Buy bus tickets at *rodoviárias* (most now take credit cards), not from travel agents who add on surcharges. Reliable bus information is hard to come by, other than from companies themselves. Buses usually arrive and depart in very good time. Many town buses have turnstiles, which can be inconvenient if you are carrying a large pack. Urban buses normally serve local airports.

Car hire Renting a car in Brazil is expensive: the cheapest rate for unlimited mileage for a small car is about US$65 per day. These costs can be more than halved by reserving a car over the internet through one of the larger international companies such as **Europcar** (www.europcar.co.uk) or **Avis** (www. avis.co.uk). The minimum age for renting a car is 21 and it's essential to have a credit card. Companies operate under the terms *aluguel de automóveis* or *auto-locadores*. Check exactly what the company's insurance policy covers. In many cases it will not cover major accidents or 'natural' damage (eg flooding). Ask if extra cover is available. Sometimes using a credit card automatically includes insurance. Beware of being billed for scratches that were on the vehicle before you hired it.

Taxi Rates vary from city to city, but are consistent within each city. At the outset, make sure the meter is cleared and shows 'tariff 1', except (usually) from 2300-0600, Sunday, and in December when '2' is permitted. Check that the meter is working; if not, fix the price in advance. The **radio taxi** service costs about 50% more but cheating is less likely. Taxis outside larger hotels usually cost more. If you are seriously cheated, note the number of the taxi and insist on a signed bill; threatening to take it to the police can work. **Mototaxis** are much more economical, but many are unlicensed and there have been a number of robberies of passengers.

Where to stay in Rio de Janeiro

There is a good range of accommodation options in Brazil. An *albergue* or hostel offers the cheapest option. These have dormitory beds and single and double rooms. Many are part of the IYHA ① *www.iyha.org*. Hostel World ① *www. hostelworld.com*; Hostel Bookers ① *www.hostelbookers.com*; and Hostel.com ① *www.hostel.com*, are useful portals. Hostel Trail Latin America ① *T0131-208 0007 (UK), www.hosteltrail.com*, managed from their hostel in Popayan, is an online network of hotels and tour companies in South America. A *pensão* is either a cheap guesthouse or a household that rents out some rooms.

Pousadas

A *pousada* is either a bed-and-breakfast, often small and family-run, or a sophisticated and often charming small hotel. A *hotel* is as it is anywhere else in the world, operating according to the international star system, although five-star hotels are not price controlled and hotels in any category are not always of the standard of their star equivalent in the USA, Canada or Europe. Many of the older hotels can be cheaper than hostels. Usually accommodation prices include a breakfast of rolls, ham, cheese, cakes and fruit with coffee and juice; there is no reduction if you don't eat it. Rooms vary too. Normally an *apartamento* is a room with separate living and sleeping areas and sometimes cooking facilities. A *quarto* is a standard room; *com banheiro* is en suite; and *sem banheiro* is with shared bathroom. Finally there are the *motels*. These should not be confused with their US counterpart: motels are used by guests not intending to sleep; there is no stigma attached and they usually offer good value (the rate for a full night is called the '*pernoite*'), however the decor can be a little garish.

It's a good idea to book accommodation in advance in small towns that are popular at weekends with city dwellers (eg near Rio de Janeiro), and it's essential to book at peak times. Hidden Pousadas Brazil ① *www.hiddenpousadasbrazil. com*, offers a range of the best *pousadas* around the country.

Luxury accommodation

Much of the best private accommodation sector can be booked through operators. Angatu, www.angatu.com, offers the best private homes along the Costa Verde, together with bespoke trips. Matuete, www.matuete.com, has a range of luxurious properties and tours throughout Brazil.

Price codes

Hotels

$$$$	over US$150	**$$$**	US$66-150
$$	US$30-65	**$**	under US$30

Price of a double room in high season, including taxes.

Restaurants

$$$	over US$12	**$$**	US$7-12	**$**	US$6 and under

Prices for a two-course meal for one person, excluding drinks or service charge.

Camping

Those with an international camping card pay only half the rate of a non-member at **Camping Clube do Brasil** sites ⓘ *www.campingclube.com.br*. Membership of the club itself is expensive: US$90 for six months. The club has 43 sites in 13 states and 80,000 members. It may be difficult to get into some Camping Clube campsites during high season (January to February). Private campsites charge about US$10-15 per person. For those on a very low budget and in isolated areas where there is no campsite available, it's usually possible to stay at service stations. They have shower facilities, watchmen and food; some have dormitories. There are also various municipal sites. Campsites tend to be some distance from public transport routes and are better suited to people with their own car. Wild camping is generally difficult and dangerous. Never camp at the side of a road; this is very risky.

Homestays

Staying with a local family is an excellent way to become integrated quickly into a city and companies try to match guests to their hosts. **Cama e Café** ⓘ *www.camaecafe.com.br*, organizes homestays in Rio de Janeiro and a number of other cities around Brazil. **Couch surfing** ⓘ *www.couchsurfing.com*, offers a free, backpacker alternative.

Quality hotel associations

The better international hotel associations have members in Brazil. These include: **Small Luxury Hotels of the World** ⓘ *www.slh.com*; the **Leading Hotels of the World** ⓘ *www.lhw.com*; the **Leading Small Hotels of the World** ⓘ *www.leadingsmallhotelsoftheworld.com*; **Great Small Hotels** ⓘ *www.greatsmallhotels.com*; and the French group **Relais et Chateaux** ⓘ *www.relaischateaux.com*, which also includes restaurants.

The Brazilian equivalent of these associations are **Hidden Pousadas Brazil** ⓘ *www.hiddenpousadasbrazil.com*, and their associate, the **Roteiros de**

Charme ① *www.roteirosdecharme.com.br*. Membership of these groups pretty much guarantees quality, but it is by no means comprehensive.

Online travel agencies (OTAs)
Services like www.tripadvisor.com and OTAs associated with them – such as www.hotels.com, www.expedia.com and www.venere.com, are well worth using for both reviews and for booking ahead. Hotels booked through an OTA can be up to 50% cheaper than the rack rate. Similar sites operate for hostels (though discounts are far less considerable). They include the Hostelling International site, www.hihostels.com, www.hostelbookers.com, www.hostels.com and www.hostelworld.com.

Food and drink in Rio de Janeiro

Food
While Brazil has some of the best fine dining restaurants in Latin America, everyday Brazilian cuisine – particularly in the southeast can be stolid. Mains are generally heavy, meaty and unspiced. Desserts are often very sweet. In Rio, a heady mix of international immigrants has resulted in some unusual fusion cooking and exquisite variations on French, Japanese, Portuguese, Arabic and Italian traditional techniques and dishes and the regional cooking can be a delight. However, at times it can be a struggle to find interesting food. The Brazilian staple meal generally consists of a cut of fried or barbecued meat, chicken or fish accompanied by rice, black or South American broad beans and an unseasoned salad of lettuce, grated carrot, tomato and beetroot. Condiments consist of weak chilli sauce, olive oil, salt and pepper and vinegar.

The national dish is a greasy campfire stew called *feijoada*, made by throwing jerked beef, smoked sausage, tongue and salt pork into a pot with lots of fat and beans and stewing it for hours. The resulting stew is sprinkled with fried *farofa* (manioc flour) and served with *couve* (kale) and slices of orange. The meal is washed down with *cachaça* (sugarcane rum). Most restaurants serve the *feijoada completa* for Saturday lunch (up until about 1630). Come with a very empty stomach.

Brazil's other national dish is mixed grilled meat or *churrasco*, served in vast portions off the spit by legions of rushing waiters, and accompanied by a buffet of salads, beans and mashed vegetables. *Churrascos* are served in *churrascarias* or *rodízios*. The meat is generally excellent, especially in the best *churascarias*, and the portions are unlimited, offering good value for camel-stomached carnivores able to eat one meal a day.

In remembrance of Portugal, but bizarrely for a tropical country replete with fish, Brazil is also the world's largest consumer of cod, pulled from the cold north Atlantic, salted and served in watery slabs or little balls as *bacalhau* (an appetizer/bar snack) or *petisco*. Other national *petiscos* include *kibe* (a deep-fried or baked mince with onion, mint and flour), *coxinha* (deep-fried chicken or meat in dough), *empadas* (baked puff-pastry patties with prawns, chicken, heart of palm or meat), and *tortas* (little pies with the same ingredients). When served in bakeries, *padarias* or snack bars these are collectively referred to as *salgadinhos* (savouries).

Eating cheaply

The cheapest dish is the *prato feito* or *sortido*, an excellent-value set menu usually comprising meat/chicken/fish, beans, rice, chips and salad. The *prato comercial* is similar but rather better and a bit more expensive. Portions are usually large enough for two and come with two plates. If you are on your own, you could ask for an *embalagem* (doggy bag) or a *marmita* (takeaway) and offer it to a person with no food (many Brazilians do). Many restaurants serve *comida por kilo* buffets where you serve yourself and pay for the weight of food on your plate. This is generally good value and is a good option for vegetarians. *Lanchonetes* and *padarias* (diners and bakeries) are good for cheap eats, usually serving *prato feitos*, *salgadinhos*, excellent juices and other snacks.

The main meal is usually taken in the middle of the day; cheap restaurants tend not to be open in the evening.

Drink

The national liquor is *cachaça* (also known as *pinga*), which is made from sugar-cane, and ranging from cheap supermarket and service-station fire-water, to boutique distillery and connoisseur labels from the interior of Minas Gerais. Mixed with fruit juice, sugar and crushed ice, *cachaça* becomes the principal element in a *batida*, a refreshing but deceptively powerful drink. Served with pulped lime or other fruit, mountains of sugar and smashed ice it becomes the world's favourite party cocktail, caipirinha. A less potent caipirinha made with vodka is called a *caipiroska* and with sake a *saikirinha* or *caipisake*.

Some genuine Scotch whisky brands are bottled in Brazil. They are far cheaper even than duty free; Teacher's is the best. Locally made and cheap gin, vermouth and campari are pretty much as good as their US and European counterparts.

Wine is becoming increasingly popular and Brazil is the third most important wine producer in South America. The wine industry is mainly concentrated in the south of the country where the conditions are most suitable, with over 90% of wine produced in Rio Grande do Sul. Reasonable national table wines include Château d'Argent, Château Duvalier, Almadén, Dreher, Preciosa and more respectable Bernard Taillan, Marjolet from Cabernet grapes, and the Moselle-type white Zahringer. There are some interesting sparkling wines in the Italian spumante style (the best is Casa Valduga Brut Premium Sparkling Wine), and

Brazil produces still wines using many international and imported varieties. The best bottle of red is probably the Boscato Reserva Cabernet Sauvignon, but it's expensive (at around US$20 a bottle); you'll get far higher quality and better value buying Portuguese, Argentine or Chilean wines in Brazil.

Brazilian beer is generally lager, served ice-cold. Draught beer is called *chope* or *chopp* (after the German Schoppen, and pronounced 'shoppi'). There are various national brands of bottled beers, which include Brahma, Skol, Cerpa, Antartica and the best Itaipava and Bohemia. There are black beers too, notably Xingu. They tend to be sweet. The best beer is from the German breweries in Rio Grande do Sul and is available only there.

Brazil's myriad fruits are used to make fruit juices or *sucos*, which come in a delicious variety, unrivalled anywhere in the world. *Açai acerola, caju* (cashew), *pitanga, goiaba* (guava), *genipapo, graviola* (chirimoya), *maracujá* (passion fruit), *sapoti, umbu* and *tamarindo* are a few of the best. *Vitaminas* are thick fruit or vegetable drinks with milk. *Caldo de cana* is sugar-cane juice, sometimes mixed with ice. *Água de côco* or *côco verde* is coconut water served straight from a chilled, fresh, green coconut. The best known of many local soft drinks is *guaraná*, which is a very popular carbonated fruit drink, completely unrelated to the Amazon nut. The best variety is *guaraná Antarctica*. Coffee is ubiquitous and good tea entirely absent.

Essentials A-Z

Accident and emergency
Ambulance T192. **Police** T190.
If robbed or attacked, contact the tourist police. If you need to claim on insurance, make sure you get a police report.

Electricity
Generally 110 V 60 cycles AC, but in some cities and areas 220 V 60 cycles AC is used. European and US 2-pin plugs and sockets.

Embassies and consulates
For embassies and consulates of Brazil, see www.embassiesabroad.com.

Health
→ *Hospitals/medical services are listed in the Directory sections of each chapter.*
See your GP or travel clinic at least 6 weeks before departure for general advice on travel risks and vaccinations. Make sure you have sufficient medical travel insurance, get a dental check, know your own blood group and, if you suffer a long-term condition such as diabetes or epilepsy, obtain a **Medic Alert** bracelet (www.medicalalert.co.uk).

Vaccinations and anti-malarials
Confirm that your primary courses and boosters are up to date. It is advisable to vaccinate against polio, tetanus, typhoid, hepatitis A and, for more remote areas, rabies. Yellow fever vaccination is obligatory for most areas. Cholera, diptheria and hepatitis B vaccinations are sometimes advised. Seek specialist advice on the best antimalarials to take before you leave.

Health risks
The major risks posed in the region are those caused by insect disease carriers such as mosquitoes and sandflies.
The key parasitic and viral diseases are malaria, South American trypanosomiasis (Chagas disease) and dengue fever. Be aware that you are always at risk from these diseases. **Malaria** is a danger throughout the lowland tropics and coastal regions. **Dengue fever** (which is currently rife in Rio de Janeiro state) is particularly hard to protect against as the mosquitoes can bite throughout the day as well as night (unlike those that carry malaria); try to wear clothes that cover arms and legs and also use effective mosquito repellent. Mosquito nets dipped in permethrin provide a good physical and chemical barrier at night. **Chagas disease** is spread by faeces of the triatomine, or assassin bugs, whereas sandflies spread a disease of the skin called **leishmaniasis**.
Some form of **diarrhoea** or intestinal upset is almost inevitable, the standard advice is always to wash your hands before eating and to be careful with drinking water and ice; if you have any doubts about the water then boil it or filter and treat it. In a restaurant buy bottled water or ask where the water has come from. Food can also pose a problem, be wary of

salads if you don't know if it has been washed or not.

There is a constant threat of **tuberculosis** (TB) and although the BCG vaccine is available, it is still not guaranteed protection. It is best to avoid unpasteurized dairy products and try not to let people cough and splutter all over you.

Another risk, especially to campers and people with small children, is that of the **hanta virus**, which is carried by some forest and riverine rodents. Symptoms are a flu-like illness which can lead to complications. Try to avoid rodent-infested areas, especially close contact with droppings.

Money
Currency ➔ *£1 = 3.8; €1 = 3.2; US$1 = R$2.3 (Jan 2014).*
The unit of currency is the **real**, R$ (plural **reais**). Any amount of foreign currency and 'a reasonable sum' in reais can be taken in, but sums over US$10,000 must be declared. Residents may only take out the equivalent of US$4000. Notes in circulation are: 100, 50, 10, 5 and 1 real; coins: 1 real, 50, 25, 10, 5 and 1 centavo. **Note** The exchange rate fluctuates – check regularly.

Costs of travelling
Brazil is more expensive than other countries in South America. As a very rough guide, prices are about two-thirds those of Western Europe and a little cheaper than rural USA.

Hostel beds are usually around US$15. Budget hotels with few frills have rooms for as little as US$30,

and you should have no difficulty finding a double room costing US$45 wherever you are. Rooms are often pretty much the same price whether 1 or 2 people are staying. Eating is generally inexpensive, especially in *padarias* or *comida por kilo* (pay by weight) restaurants, which offer a wide range of food (salads, meat, pasta, vegetarian). Expect to pay around US$6 to eat your fill in a good-value restaurant. Although bus travel is cheap by US or European standards, because of the long distances, costs can soon mount up. Internal flights prices have come down dramatically in the last couple of years and some routes work out cheaper than taking a bus – especially if booking through the internet. Prices vary regionally. Ipanema is almost twice as expensive as rural Bahia.

ATMs
ATMs, or cash machines, are common in Brazil. As well as being the most convenient way of withdrawing money, they frequently offer the best available rates of exchange. They are usually closed after 2130 in large cities. There are 2 international ATM acceptance systems, **Plus** and **Cirrus**. Many issuers of debit and credit cards are linked to one, or both (eg Visa is Plus, MasterCard is Cirrus). **Bradesco** and **HSBC** are the 2 main banks offering this service. **Red Banco 24 Horas** kiosks advertise that they take a long list of credit cards in their ATMs, including MasterCard and Amex, but international cards cannot always be used; the same is true of **Banco do Brasil**.

Advise your bank before leaving, as cards are usually stopped in Brazil without prior warning. Find out before you leave what international functionality your card has. Check if your bank or credit card company imposes handling charges. Internet banking is useful for monitoring your account or transferring funds. Do not rely on one card, in case of loss. If you do lose a card, immediately contact the 24-hr helpline of the issuer in your home country (keep this number in a safe place).

Exchange

Banks in major cities will change cash and traveller's cheques (TCs). If you keep the official exchange slips, you may convert back into foreign currency up to 50% of the amount you exchanged. The parallel market, found in travel agencies, exchange houses and among hotel staff, often offers marginally better rates than the banks but commissions can be very high. Many banks may only change US$300 minimum in cash, US$500 in TCs. Rates for TCs are usually far lower than for cash, they are harder to change and a very heavy commission may be charged.

Credit cards

Credit cards are widely used, athough often they are not usable in the most unlikely of places, such as tour operators. **Diners Club**, **MasterCard**, **Visa** and **Amex** are useful. Cash advances on credit cards will only be paid in reais at the tourist rate, incurring at least a 1.5% commission.

Banks in remote places may refuse to give a cash advance: try asking for the *gerente* (manager).

Opening hours

Generally Mon-Fri 0900-1800; closed for lunch sometime between 1130 and 1400. **Shops** Also open on Sat until 1230 or 1300. **Government offices** Mon-Fri 1100-1800. **Banks** Mon-Fri 1000-1600 or 1630; closed at weekends.

Safety

Although Brazil's big cities suffer high rates of violent crime, this is mostly confined to the *favelas* (slums) where poverty and drugs are the main cause. Visitors should not enter *favelas* except when accompanied by workers for NGOs, tour groups or other people who know the local residents well and are accepted by the community. Otherwise they may be targets of muggings by armed gangs who show short shrift to those who resist them. Mugging can take place anywhere. Travel light after dark with few valuables (avoid wearing jewellery and use a cheap, plastic, digital watch). Ask hotel staff where is and isn't safe; crime is patchy in Brazilian cities.

If the worst does happen and you are threatened, don't panic, and hand over your valuables. Do not resist, and report the crime to the local tourist police later. It is extremely rare for a tourist to be hurt during a robbery in Brazil. Being aware of the dangers, acting confidently and using your common sense will reduce many of the risks.

Photocopy your passport, air ticket and other documents, make a record of traveller's cheque and credit card numbers. Keep them separately from the originals and leave another set of records at home. Keep all documents secure; hide your main cash supply in different places or under your clothes. Extra pockets sewn inside shirts and trousers, money belts (best worn below the waist), neck or leg pouches and elasticated support bandages for keeping money above the elbow or below the knee have been repeatedly recommended.

All border areas should be regarded with some caution because of smuggling activities. Violence over land ownership in parts of the interior have resulted in a 'Wild West' atmosphere in some towns, which should therefore be passed through quickly. Red-light districts should also be given a wide berth as there are reports of drinks being drugged with a substance popularly known as 'good night Cinderella'. This leaves the victim easily amenable to having their possessions stolen, or worse.

Avoiding cons

Never trust anyone telling sob stories or offering 'safe rooms', and when looking for a hotel, always choose the room yourself. Be wary of 'plain-clothes policemen'; insist on seeing identification and on going to the police station by main roads. Do not hand over your identification (or money) until you are at the station. On no account take them directly back to your hotel. Be even more suspicious if

they seek confirmation of their status from a passer-by.

Hotel security

Hotel safe deposits are generally, but not always, secure. If you cannot get a receipt for valuables in a hotel safe, you can seal the contents in a plastic bag and sign across the seal. Always keep an inventory of what you have deposited. If you don't trust the hotel, lock everything in your pack and secure it in your room when you go out. If you lose valuables, report to the police and note details of the report for insurance purposes. Be sure to be present whenever your credit card is used.

Police

There are several types of police: **Polícia Federal**, civilian dressed, who handle all federal law duties, including immigration. A subdivision is the **Polícia Federal Rodoviária**, uniformed, who are the traffic police on federal highways. **Polícia Militar** are the uniformed, street police force, under the control of the state governor, handling all state laws. They are not the same as the Armed Forces' internal police. **Polícia Civil**, also state controlled, handle local laws and investigations. They are usually in civilian dress, unless in the traffic division. In cities, the *prefeitura* controls the **Guarda Municipal**, who handle security. **Tourist police** operate in places with a strong tourist presence. In case of difficulty, visitors should seek out tourist police in the first instance.

Public transport

When you have all your luggage with you at a bus or railway station, be especially careful and carry any shoulder bags in front of you. To be extra safe, take a taxi between the airport/bus station/railway station and hotel, keep your bags with you and pay only when you and your luggage are outside; avoid night buses and arriving at your destination at night.

Sexual assault

If you are the victim of a sexual assault, you are advised firstly to contact a doctor (this can be your home doctor). You will need tests to determine whether you have contracted any STDs; you may also need advice on emergency contraception. You should contact your embassy, where consular staff will be very willing to help.

Telephone → *Country code: +55.*
Ringing: equal tones with long pauses. Engaged: equal tones, equal pauses.

Making a phone call in Brazil can be confusing. It is necessary to dial a 2-digit telephone company code prior to the area code for all calls. Phone numbers are now printed in this way: 0XX21 (0 for a national call, XX for the code of the phone company chosen (eg 31 for Telemar) followed by, 21 for Rio de Janeiro, for example, and the 8-digit number of the subscriber. The same is true for international calls where 00 is followed by the operator code and then the country code and number.

Time

Brazilian standard time is GMT-3. Clocks move forward 1 hr in summer for approximately 5 months (usually between Oct and Feb or Mar), but times of change vary.

Tipping

Tipping is not usual, but always appreciated as staff are often paid a pittance. In restaurants, add 10% of the bill if no service charge is included; cloakroom attendants deserve a small tip; porters have fixed charges but often receive tips as well; unofficial car parkers on city streets should be tipped R$2.

Tourist information

The **Ministério do Turismo**, Esplanada dos Ministérios, Bloco U, 2nd and 3rd floors, Brasília, www.turismo.gov.br or www.braziltour.com, is in charge of tourism in Brazil and has information in many languages. **Embratur**, the Brazilian Institute of Tourism, is at the same address, and is in charge of promoting tourism abroad. For information and phone numbers for your country visit **www.braziltour. com**. Local tourist information bureaux are not usually helpful for information on cheap hotels – they generally just dish out pamphlets. Expensive hotels provide tourist magazines for their guests. Telephone directories (not Rio) contain good street maps.

Other good sources of information are:
LATA, www.lata.org. The Latin American Travel Association, with

useful country information and listings of all UK operators specializing in Latin America. Also has up-to-date information on public safety, health, weather, travel costs, economics and politics highlighted for each nation. Wide selection of Latin American maps available, as well as individual travel planning assistance.

South American Explorers, formerly the **South American Explorers Club**, 126 Indina Creek Rd, Ithaca, NY 14850, T607-277 0488, www.samexplo.org. A non-profit educational organization functioning primarily as an information network for South America.

National parks

National parks are run by the Brazilian institute of environmental protection, **Ibama**, SCEN Trecho 2, Av L-4 Norte, Edif Sede de Ibama, CEP 70818-900, Brasília, DF, T061-3316 1212, www.ibama.gov.br. For information, contact **Linha Verde**, T0800-618080, linhaverde.sede@ibama.gov.br. National parks are open to visitors, usually with a permit from Ibama. See also the **Ministério do Meio Ambiente** website, www.mma.gov.br.

Visas and immigration

Visas are not required for stays of up to 90 days by tourists from Andorra, Argentina, Austria, Bahamas, Barbados, Belgium, Bolivia, Chile, Colombia, Costa Rica, Denmark, Ecuador, Finland, France, Germany, Greece, Iceland, Ireland, Italy, Liechtenstein, Luxembourg, Malaysia, Monaco, Morocco, Namibia, the Netherlands, Norway, Paraguay, Peru, Philippines,

Portugal, San Marino, South Africa, Spain, Suriname, Sweden, Switzerland, Thailand, Trinidad and Tobago, United Kingdom, Uruguay, the Vatican and Venezuela. For them, only the following documents are required at the port of disembarkation: a passport valid for at least 6 months (or *cédula de identidad* for nationals of Argentina, Chile, Paraguay and Uruguay); and a return or onward ticket, or adequate proof that you can purchase your return fare, subject to no remuneration being received in Brazil and no legally binding or contractual documents being signed. Venezuelan passport holders can stay for 60 days on filling in a form at the border.

Citizens of the USA, Canada, Australia, New Zealand and other countries not mentioned above, and anyone wanting to stay longer than 180 days, *must* get a visa before arrival, which may, if you ask, be granted for multiple entry. US citizens must be fingerprinted on entry to Brazil. Visa fees vary from country to country, so apply to the Brazilian consulate in your home country. The consular fee in the USA is US$55. Students planning to study in Brazil or employees of foreign companies can apply for a 1- or 2-year visa. 2 copies of the application form, 2 photos, a letter from the sponsoring company or educational institution in Brazil, a police form showing no criminal convictions and a fee of around US$80 is required.

Identification

You must always carry identification when in Brazil. Take a photocopy of the personal details in your passport, plus your Brazilian immigration stamp, and leave your passport in the hotel safe deposit. This photocopy, when authorized in a *cartório*, US$1, is a legitimate copy of your documents. Be prepared, however, to present the originals when travelling in sensitive border areas. Always keep an independent record of your passport details. Also register with your consulate to expedite document replacement if yours gets lost or stolen.

Warning Do not lose the entry/exit permit they give you when you enter Brazil. Leaving the country without it, you may have to pay up to US$100 per person. It is suggested that you photocopy this form and have it authenticated at a *cartório*, US$1, in case of loss or theft.

Weights and measures
Metric.

Contents

Footprint features

At a glance

⊖ **Getting around** Bus, *metrô*
and taxi. Hiring a car is
recommended for visiting
the more remote areas in
Rio state but not for the city.

◔ **Time required** At least
3 days to explore the city;
7-10 days for the city and state.

☼ **Weather** Summer (Dec-Mar)
is warm and wet, up to 30°C;
winter (Apr-Oct) is dry with
blue skies.

✖ **When not to go** Good at
any time but wet Dec-Jan.
Hotel prices double over
New Year and Carnaval.

Rio de Janeiro

Rio de Janeiro city

According to Cariocas – the people of Rio de Janeiro – God made the world in six days and then spent the seventh lying on the beach in Ipanema. For in a city as beautiful as this, they say, only the philistine or the ungrateful would do anything else. Indeed, photographs cannot prepare you for Rio. There is far more to the city than Corcovado capped with Christ or the Sugar Loaf; these are overtures to the grand symphony of the scene. Rainforest-covered boulder mountains as high as Snowdon rise sheer from the sea around the vast Guanabara Bay and stretch to the horizon. Their curves and jags are broken by long sweeping beaches of powder-fine sand pounded by the dazzling green ocean, or by perfect half-moon coves lapped by the gentle waters of the bay. The city clusters around them, climbing over hills and crowding behind beaches and lakes. Its neighbourhoods are connected by tunnels bored through the ancient rock or across winding double-decker highways that cling vertiginously to the cliffs above the fierce Atlantic Ocean.

Against this magical backdrop, the famous Carioca day leisurely unwinds. When the sun is up the middle classes head for the beach, wearing nothing but tiny speedos or bikinis. Here they surf, play beach volleyball or football, or soak up the rays between occasional dips into the waves, with the working day just a brief interruption. When the sun is down, still wearing almost nothing, they head for the *botecos* (street bars) for an ice-cold draught beer or *chope*. Then they go home, finally put some clothes on and prepare to go out until the early hours of the morning.

Getting there

Air Rio is served by two airports. **Aeroporto Internacional Tom Jobim**
ⓘ Ilha *do Governador, 15 km north of the city centre, www.aeroporto
galeao.net* (formerly known as Galeão and often still called by this name),
receives international and domestic flights. There are *câmbios* in the departure
hall and on the first floor of international arrivals. The **Banco do Brasil** on
the third floor (open 24 hours) has better rates of exchange. There are also
ATMs for major Brazilian banks, several of which accept Visa and MasterCard.
Duty-free shops are well stocked and open to arrivals as well as departures.
There are **Riotur** information booths in the domestic arrivals hall of **Terminal
1** ⓘ *T021-3398 4077, daily 0600-2300*, and in the international arrivals hall
in **Terminal 2** ⓘ *T021-3398 2245, daily 0600-2400*, which provide maps and
can book accommodation. **Santos Dumont Airport** ⓘ *in the city centre on
Guanabara Bay, www.aeroportosantosdumont.net*, is used for Rio–São Paulo
shuttle flights (see Transport, page 97), a handful of other domestic routes,
private planes or air taxis. For more information visit www.infraero.gov.br and
click on 'aeroportos'.

Taxis can be booked from within the airports or picked up at the stands
outside the terminals. Fixed-rate taxis charge around US$32 from Jobim to
Copacabana or Ipanema and US$30 to the city centre or Santa Teresa (about
half as much from Santos Dumont); buy a ticket at the counter. **Aerotaxi cabs**
ⓘ *T021-2467 1500, available outside both terminals at Tom Jobim Airport cost
US$25 (plus US$0.75 per item of luggage)*. Metered taxis cost around US$30
from Jobim to Copacabana, but beware of pirate taxis, which are unlicensed.
Fixed-price taxis leave from the first floor of both terminals and have clearly
marked booths selling tickets.

There are frequent buses between the two airports, the *rodoviária* (interstate
bus station) and the city; the best are the air-conditioned **Real Auto** ⓘ *T0800-
240850, www.realautoonibus.com.br*, which leave from outside arrivals on
the first floor of terminals 1 and 2 at Tom Jobim (aka Galeão) and run 0500-
2400, US$5. There are two routes: *Linha 2018 via Orla da Zona Sul*, runs every
30 minutes, to the Terminal Alvorada bus station in Barra da Tijuca and back
again, stopping at the *rodoviária*, Avenida Rio Branco in the centre, Santos
Dumont airport, Flamengo, Copacabana, Ipanema, São Conrado and Barra's
Avenida das Americas. (This should not be confused with the *Linha 2018 via
Linha Vermelha*, which runs a sporadic circular route via Barra and nowhere
else of any use to foreign tourists.) *Linha 2145*, runs every 25 minutes to Santos
Dumont Airport and back again, calling at Avenida Rio Branco along the way.
Buses can be flagged down anywhere along their route and passengers can
request to jump off at any time. There is also a standard Rio bus running along

1 Rio de Janeiro

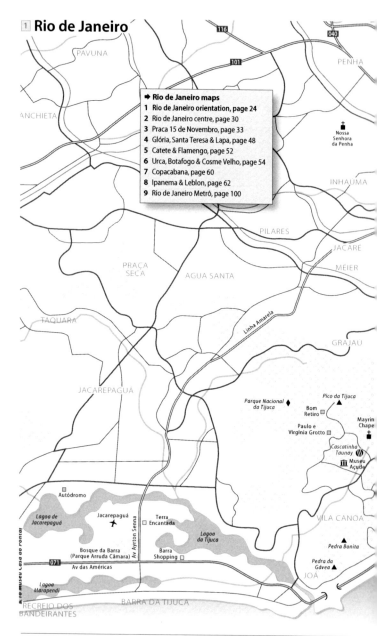

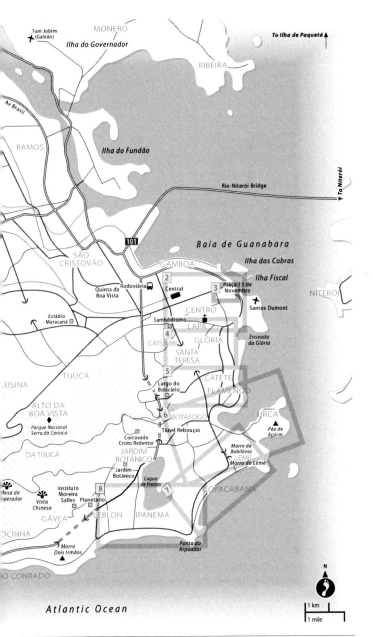

the 2018 line with similar frequency, US$2. Ordinary city buses also run from the airport to various locations in Rio, from the first floor of both terminals. These are far less secure and are not recommended. ▸▸ *See Transport, page 97.*

Bus International and interstate buses arrive at the newly renovated **Rodoviária Novo Rio** ⓘ *Av Francisco Bicalho 01 at Rodrigues Alves, Santo Cristo, T021-3213 1800, www.novorio.com.br.* There is a **Riotur** ⓘ *T021-2263 4857, daily 0700-1900,* information centre, which can help with orientation and accommodation. Left luggage costs US$5. There are *câmbios* (cash only) and ATMs. From the *rodoviária* it is best to take a taxi to your hotel or to the nearest *metrô* station (Metrô Estácio); taxis can be booked at the booth on the ground floor. The *metrô* runs south as far as Copacabana (Metrô Cantagalo); for Ipanema and Leblon head to Metrô Siqueira Campos and take a taxi from there, or take bus marked 'Metrô-Gávea'.

The **local bus terminal** is just outside the *rodoviária*: turn right as you leave and run the gauntlet of taxi drivers. The bus station attracts thieves, so exercise caution. The air-conditioned **Real** bus (opposite the exit) goes along the beach to São Conrado and will secure luggage. If you need a taxi collect a ticket from the office inside the entrance as this protects against over-charging; a taxi to Flamengo costs approximately US$15.

Getting around
The city is made up of separate districts connected by urban highways and tunnels heavy with traffic, so it's best to use public transport or taxis to get around. An underground railway, the **metrô** ⓘ *T0800-2595 1111, www. metrorio.com.br, Mon-Sat 0500-2400, Sun and holidays 0700-2300 and 24 hrs during Carnaval, tickets R$3.50/US$1.75 (for a one-way journey and for the connecting 'Metrô na Superficie' Gávea/Barra express bus which passes through Ipanema and Leblon),* runs from the outer suburbs of the Zona Norte, through the city centre (including the Sambódromo and the Maracanã stadium), Glória, Flamengo, Botafogo, Copacabana, the Lagoa to the Arpoador end of Ipanema. The Metrô-Barra buses connect at the penultimate station – General Osório (aka Tom Jobim or Ipanema) – for Leblon, Gávea and Barra. The *metrô* is currently undergoing expansion with sporadic station closures in Copacabana and Ipanema. By the 2016 Olympics, the service will extend to Rocinha, São Conrado and Barra da Tijuca. *Metrô* stations often have a number of different access points. **Buses** (R$2.70/US$1.35 per journey, see www.rioonibus.com for a full list of bus lines) run to all parts, but should be treated with caution at night, when taxis or minivans are a better bet. Buses are usually marked with the destination and any going south of the centre will call at Copacabana and generally Ipanema/Leblon. **Minivans** (R$2.50/US$1.25 per journey) run from Avenida Rio Branco in the centre as far south as Barra da Tijuca and have

the destination written on the window. They are fast, frequent and by far the cheapest way of getting along the beaches. These vans also run along the sea front from Leme to Rocinha and can be hailed from the kerb. **Taxis** should always be booked through a hostel or hotel, or caught from a designated taxi *posto*; the name of the *posto* should be written in navy blue on the side of the taxi. Be wary of freelance taxis hailed in the street or those without a taxi rank inscription. Taxis from Glória *metrô* to Santa Teresa cost around US$5. The famous yellow Santa Teresa **trams** are currently not running following a serious accident in 2011. They are due to start running again in time for the Olympics. The route runs from the Largo da Carioca, near the *metrô* station and the cathedral, passing over the Lapa viaduct and running along all the main streets in Santa Teresa (via the Largo do Guimarães and Largo das Neves), and eventually reaching either Dois Irmãos or Paula Mattos at the far end of Santa Teresa (see page 47).

Tourist information

Riotur ⓘ *Praça Pio X, 119, 9th floor, Centro, T021-2271 7000, www.rioguiaoficial. com.br*, is the city's government tourist office. There are also booths or offices in **Copacabana** ⓘ *Centro de Atendimento ao Turista, Av Princesa Isabel 183, T021-2541 7522, Mon-Fri 0900-1800*, and **Copacabana Posto Seis** ⓘ *Av Rainha Elizabeth 36 at NS de Copacabana, T021-2513 0077, Mon-Fri 0900-1800*. The helpful staff speak English, French and German and can provide good city maps and a very useful free brochure. There are further information stands at **Corcovado** ⓘ *R Cosme Velho 513, T021-2258 1329 ext 4, on the upper and lower levels of the elevator*, and at the international airport and Novo Rio bus station. There is also a free telephone information service, **Alô Rio** ⓘ *T021-2542 8080 or T021-2542 8004*, in Portuguese and English.

The state tourism organization is **Turisrio** ⓘ *R da Ajuda 5, 6th floor, Centro, T021-2215 0011, www.turisrio.rj.gov.br, Mon-Fri 0900-1800*. The private sector **Rio Convention and Visitors Bureau** ⓘ *R Visconde de Pirajá 547, suite 610, Ipanema, T021-2259 6165, www.rioconventionbureau.com.br*, also offers information and assistance in English. **Embratur** ⓘ *R Uruguaiana 174, 8th floor, Centro, T021-2509 6017, www.visitbrasil.com*, provides information on the whole country.

Background

The coast of Rio de Janeiro was first settled about 5000 years ago by tribal peoples who arrived in South America either through the Bering Islands or possibly across the Pacific. When the Europeans arrived, the indigenous inhabitants belonged to the Tupi or Tupi-Guarani, Botocudos, Puri and

Maxacali linguistic groups. Tragically, no indigenous people in this region survived the European incursions.

The Portuguese navigator, **Gonçalo Coelho**, landed at what is now Rio de Janeiro on 1 January 1502. Mistaking the Baía de Guanabara (the name the local people used) to be the mouth of a great river, they called it the 'January River'. But the bay wasn't settled until 1555 when the French, under the Huguenot Admiral Nicholas Durand de Villegagnon, occupied Lage Island. They later transferred to Seregipe Island (now Villegagnon), where they built the fort of Coligny. The fort has been demolished to make way for the Escola Naval (naval college), and the island itself, since the narrow channel was filled up, has become a part of the mainland. Villegagnon set up a colony as the starting point for what he called Antarctic France.

In 1559-1560, Mem de Sá, the third governor of Brazil, mounted an expedition from Salvador to attack the French, who were supported by the indigenous Tamoio. The Portuguese succeeded in capturing the French fort and putting an end to Antarctic France, but did not colonize the area until 1567 when they transferred their settlement to the Morro de São Januário. This is generally considered the date of the founding of the city of São Sebastião do Rio de Janeiro, so called in honour of the Portuguese prince who would soon assume the throne.

Though constantly attacked by local indigenous groups, the new city grew rapidly and when King Sebastião divided Brazil into two provinces, Rio was chosen as capital of the southern captaincies. Salvador became sole capital again in 1576, but Rio again became the southern capital in 1608 and the seat of a bishopric. There was a further French incursion in 1710-1711 as a result of the tension between France and Portugal during the war of Spanish Succession, and because of the flow of gold out of Minas Gerais through Rio. Rio de Janeiro was by now becoming the leading city in Brazil. Not only was it the port out of which gold was shipped, but it was also the focus of the export/import trade of the surrounding agricultural lands. On 27 January 1763, it became the seat of the viceroy. After Independence, in 1834, it was declared capital of the empire and remained so for 125 years.

The shaping of a city

Rio went from a colonial capital to the capital of a large empire when King João and the entire Portuguese court fled to Brazil in 1808 in fear of Napoleon, abandoning Portugal to a caretaker British Army General. The ideas they brought with them from Europe began to transform Rio. New formal gardens and stately *praças*, graced with faux-European fountains were built to accommodate the court's more refined tastes and lavish mansions and palaces were built to house the royals and their retinue. Despite his fear of Napoleon, King João invited an artistic mission from France to found academies of fine art and music in Rio in 1816. The architect Grandjean de Montigny, the painter Jean-Baptiste Debret and sculptor Nicolas Antoine Taunay began an artistic relationship which continued into the 20th century through Le Corbusier and Levi-Strauss and which provided the template for modern Brazil's artistic and academic development. The city also expanded geographically, growing north into São Cristóvão and Tijuca and south through Glória, Catete, Flamengo and Botafogo. It also grew in prosperity, with wealthy coffee barons building *chacaras* (country houses) in the hills around Tijuca and Santa Teresa – a trend which continued into Independence. By the time Brazil had become a republic in 1889, Rio was by far the most important city in the country politically, culturally and economically.

The new republic was founded on French positivist principles, which were resolutely pragmatic and functionalist, as expressed by the new national motto 'Order and Progress'. The past was discarded; sadly it included much of colonial Rio whose beautiful terracotta tiled roofs, old alleys, churches and mansion houses were razed to the ground and replaced by poor versions of US office blocks, lining broad new avenues such as the 33-m-wide Avenida Central (later renamed Avenida Rio Branco). The disenfranchised poor Brazilian majority, many of whom were recently freed African-Brazilian slaves refused work on the plantations, began to cluster on the hills in ungainly shanty towns, or *favelas*.

In 1960 Brazil entered an era of Order and Progress when new president Juscelino Kubitschek declared that his country would leap 50 years in just five – equivalent to his term of office. JK shifted the nation's capital several thousand kilometres inland to the new purpose-built Jetson-age Brasília, sending the country into bankruptcy and Rio into decline. The commercial centre crumbled, the bright lights of Lapa and Cinelândia flickered and went dim and wealthy Cariocas left for the beaches around Ipanema and São Conrado. Resurrection began in the 1990s, when a new mayor, Luiz Paulo Conde, embarked on a massive programme of regeneration, remodelling the bay-side suburbs and attracting residents, artistic endeavours and small businesses to neglected districts. Lapa re-emerged as a nightlife centre and Rio began to find its cultural feet again. But years of neglect had left a toll. Contemporary Rio has hundreds of *favelas* and a population chronically divided between the haves, who live in the Cidade Maravilhosa, and the have-nots, who live in the Cidade de Deus or similar slum communities.

2 Rio de Janeiro centre

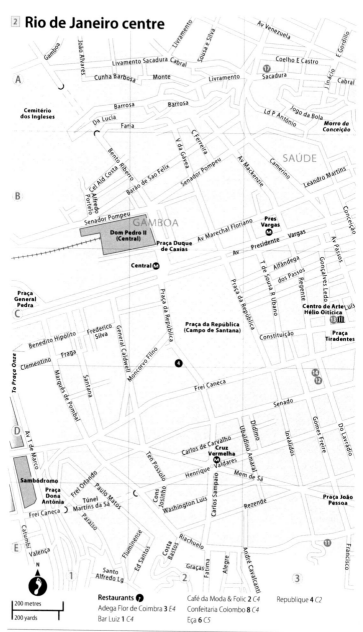

Restaurants ❼
Adega Flor de Coimbra **3** *E4*
Bar Luiz **1** *C4*

Café da Moda & Folic **2** *C4*
Confeitaria Colombo **8** *C4*
Eça **6** *C5*

Republique **4** *C2*

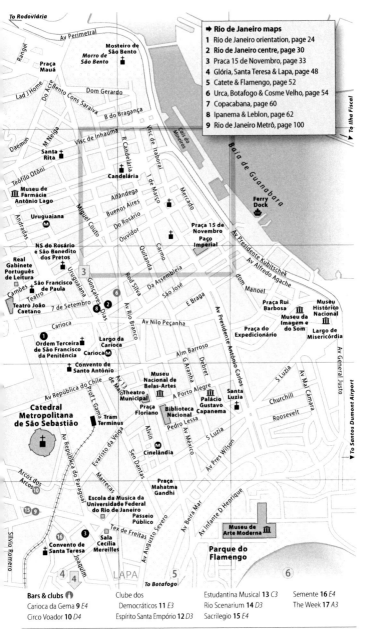

➡ Rio de Janeiro maps

1 Rio de Janeiro orientation, page 24
2 Rio de Janeiro centre, page 30
3 Praça 15 de Novembro, page 33
4 Glória, Santa Teresa & Lapa, page 48
5 Catete & Flamengo, page 52
6 Urca, Botafogo & Cosme Velho, page 54
7 Copacabana, page 60
8 Ipanema & Leblon, page 62
9 Rio de Janeiro Metrô, page 100

Central Rio and Lapa → *For listings, see pages 70-103.*

Hot and sweaty central Rio spreads back from Guanabara Bay in a jumbled grid of streets between Santos Dumont Airport and the Jesuit Mosteiro São Bento. It dates from 1567, but much of its architectural heritage has been laid waste by successive waves of government intent on wiping out the past in favour of dubious and grandiose visions of Order and Progress. Nevertheless it remains the centre of Rio's history as well as the city, with some distinguished colonial buildings, Manueline follies and elaborate neoclassical facades huddled together under totalitarian blocks of flats and Le Corbusier-inspired concrete. All watch over a mass of cars and a bustle of people: business suits on lunch, beggars, skateboarders dressed in would-be New York oversized jeans and baseball caps, street performers and opportunists looking to snatch a purse. It can all feel a bit hectic and bewildering. But don't give up. There is plenty to explore here and a wealth of air-conditioned havens in which to escape for respite and a coffee.

The greatest concentration of historic buildings is in the south of the centre, near Santos Dumont Airport and around **Praça 15 de Novembro**, from where Rio de Janeiro grew in its earliest days. Here you'll find most of the museums, some of the city's more beautiful little churches and colonial buildings such as the **Paço Imperial** and the **Palácio Tiradentes**. More colonial buildings lie at the centre's northern extremity around the Morro de São Bento. These include the finest baroque building in Rio, the **Mosteiro de São Bento**, and the city's most imposing church, **Nossa Senhora da Candelária**.

The city's main artery is the **Avenida Presidente Vargas**, 4.5 km long and more than 90 m wide, which divides these northern and southern sections. It begins at the waterfront, splits around the Candelária church, then crosses the Avenida Rio Branco in a magnificent straight stretch past the **Central do Brasil** railway station. Vargas is dissected by two important arterial streets. **Avenida Rio Branco**, nearest to the sea, was once lined with splendid ornate buildings, which were quite the equal of any in Buenos Aires. These have largely been razed to the ground but a few remain around **Cinelândia**. **Avenida 31 Março**, further to the west beyond the railway station, leads to the **Sambódromo** and the Carnaval district. Some of the better modern architecture is to be found along Avenida República do Chile, including the conical 1960s **Catedral Metropolitana de São Sebastião**.

Arriving in central Rio and Lapa

For Praça 15 de Novembro, Largo do Carioca, Cinelândia and Lapa take the *metrô* to Carioca in Cinelândia. For Candelária and São Bento take the *metrô* to Uruguiana. For the Cidade Nova and Sambódromo take the *metrô* to Praça Onze. Opening times for churches, museums and public buildings change frequently. All museums close during Carnaval.

Praça 15 de Novembro and the imperial palaces

Originally an open space at the foot of the Morro do Castelo – a hill which has now been flattened – the Praça 15 de Novembro (often called Praça Quinze) has always been one of the focal points in Rio de Janeiro. Today it has one of the greatest concentrations of historic buildings in the city. Having been through various phases of development, the area underwent major remodelling in the late 1990s. The last vestiges of the original harbour, at the seaward end of the *praça*, were restored. Avenida Alfredo Agache now goes through an underpass, creating an open space between the *praça* and the seafront and giving easy access to the ferry dock for Niterói. The area is well illuminated and clean and the municipality has started to stage shows, music and dancing in the *praça*. At weekends an antiques, crafts, stamp and coin fair (Feirarte II) is held 0900-1900. The rather modest colonial former royal palace, **Paço Imperial** ① *on the southeast corner of Praça 15 de Novembro, T021-2533 4407, www.pacoimperial. com.br, Tue-Sun 1200-1800*, is one of the centre's landmarks. It was built in 1743 as the residence of the governor of the Capitania and was made into the

➡ Rio de Janeiro maps
1 Rio de Janeiro orientation, page 24
2 Rio de Janeiro centre, page 30
3 Praça 15 de Novembro, page 33
4 Glória, Santa Teresa & Lapa, page 48
5 Catete & Flamengo, page 52
6 Urca, Botafogo & Cosme Velho, page 54
7 Copacabana, page 60
8 Ipanema & Leblon, page 62
9 Rio de Janeiro Metrô, page 100

③ **Praça 15 de Novembro**

royal palace when the Portuguese court moved to Brazil. After independence it became the imperial palace. It fell into disuse in the mid-20th century to be resurrected as a temporary exhibition space and arts centre. There's often something interesting on display here, and two decent air-conditioned café-restaurants, the **Bistro** and **Atrium**, provide respite from the heat. Just north of the palace is the **Chafariz do Mestre Valentim** (or Chafariz do Pirâmide), a fountain designed by the famous sculptor.

Beside the Paço Imperial, across Rua da Assembléia, is the grand neoclassical **Palácio Tiradentes** ① *T021-2588 1411, www.alerj.rj.gov.br, Mon-Sat 1000-1700, Sun and holidays 1200-1700, guided visits by appointment only, T021-2588 1251*. It was named in honour of the former dentist (*tiradentes* means teeth puller), Joaquim José da Silva Xavier, who is often seen as the symbolic father of Brazilian independence, and who was held prisoner here and executed nearby. The building itself was constructed between 1922 and 1926 and is now the state legislative assembly. A **statue of Tiradentes** by Francisco de Andrade stands in front.

Largo da Misericórdia and the museums

There is a cluster of interesting little museums south of Praça XV on the way to Santos Dumont Airport that can be reached by the Largo da Misericórdia, which runs immediately south of the Palácio Tiradentes. At the end of the *largo* is the **Ladeira da Misericórdia**; the oldest street in Rio and now just a severed stump on the side of the grand Santa Casa da Misericórdia hospital. This hill was once crowned by a magnificent monastery and fort that watched out over the bay. Next door to the hospital, in a series of handsome buildings, is the **Museu Histórico Nacional** ① *Praça Marechal Âncora, T021-2550 9224, www.museuhitoriconacional.com.br, Tue-Fri 1000-1700, Sat and Sun 1400-1800, US$3, free on Sun*. This is one of the city's more distinguished museums, with a collection of magnificent carriages, historical treasures, colonial sculpture and furniture, maps, paintings, arms and armour, silver and porcelain. It also retains a rampart from that first fort that crowned the former Morro do Castelo hill from the 1603 until the 20th century. The building was once the war arsenal of the empire, and was partly constructed in 1762 (this part is called the 'Casa do Trem'). The **Museu da Imagem e do Som (MIS)** ① *at the moment split between 2 centres: R Visconde de Maranguape 15, Largo da Lapa, T021-2332 9508, and Praça Luiz Souza Dantas (aka Praça Rui Barbosa) 01, Praça XV, T021-2332 9068, Mon-Fri 1100-1700, www.mis.rj.gov.br, free, visits by appointment only*, was scheduled to move into a swanky, purpose-built new building in Copacabana in 2012 but remains unopened in 2013. It currently houses a collection of cinema images, photos of Rio and of Carioca musicians, and recordings of popular music, including early *choro* by artists including Jacob do Bandolim. There are booths for listening to music and a small cinema for watching the 16 mm and 35 mm film archive.

Travessa do Comércio and the Carmelite churches

North of Praça XV, the **Travessa do Comércio** and its continuation to the left, the **Rua do Ouvidor**, are reached via the **Arco do Teles** directly across from the palace. The arch is all that remains of an 18th-century construction, now incorporated into a modern building, and the two streets give an idea of how most of Rio must have looked in the 19th century. Little bars and restaurants line the streets and are very lively after 1800. These include the **Arco Imperial**, where Carmen Miranda lived between 1925 and 1930 (her mother kept a boarding house). There are also some interesting bookshops and one of Brazil's prettiest little baroque churches, **Nossa Senhora da Lapa dos Mercadores** ① *R do Ouvidor 35, T021-2509 2239, Mon-Fri 0800-1400*. This began life as a street oratory erected in a blind alley by market vendors who traditionally petitioned Our Lady of Lapa for help in hard times; it became a church in 1750, was remodelled in 1869-1872 and has now been fully restored.

The busy thoroughfare of Rua 1 de Março cuts across the top of Praça XV and Rua Ouvidor and is littered with Carmelite churches, all of them worth a quick look. The most famous is at the northwestern corner of the *praça*: **Nossa Senhora do Carmo da Antiga Sé** ① *R 1 de Março at R 7 de Setembro 14, T021-2509 2239, Tue-Thu 0900-1700, Sat 1100-1700*, has one of the finest baroque interiors in Rio and occupies the site of the original founding Carmelite chapel, which stood here between 1590 and 1754. The current church dates from 1761. After the arrival of the Portuguese court in 1808 it became the designated Royal Chapel and subsequently the city's first cathedral – between 1900 and 1976. The crypt allegedly holds the remains of Pedro Alvares Cabral, the European discoverer of Brazil; a claim disputed by the town of Santarém in Portugal. Just north of this church and right in front of the end of Rua Ouvidor is the **Igreja da Ordem Terceira do Monte do Carmo** ① *R 1 de Março s/n, Mon-Fri 0800-1400, Sat 0800-1200*. This was built in 1754, consecrated in 1770 and rebuilt in the 19th century. It has strikingly beautiful portals by Mestre Valentim, the son of a Portuguese nobleman and a slave girl. He also created the main altar of fine moulded silver, the throne and its chair and much else. At the rear of the old cathedral and the Igreja da Ordem Terceira do Monte do Carmo, on Rua do Carmo, is the **Oratório de Nossa Senhora do Cabo da Boa Esperança**; one of the few remaining public oratories from the colonial period in Rio.

Candelária and around

Rio's most imposing church lies on an island in a sea of traffic some 500 m north of Praça XV. The mock-Italianate **Igreja de Nossa Senhora da Candelária** ① *Praça Pio X, T021-2233 2324, Mon-Fri 0800-1600, Sat 0800-1200, Sun 0900-1300*, has long been the church of 'society Rio'. Celebrities still gather here in the marble interior for the city's most prestigious weddings. The church is modelled on the Basílica da Estrela in Portugal. The tiles in the dome are from Lisbon, the marble inside is Veronan and the heavy bronze doors were commissioned from France. All were shipped across at vast expense in the late 18th century, during an era when even though such materials were readily available in Brazil at similar quality and far lower prices, snob value demanded that they be imported. The church was built on the site of a chapel founded in 1610 by the Spaniard Antônio Martins Palma who arrived in Rio after surviving a terrible storm at sea. He erected the chapel in homage to Nuestra Señora de Candelária, the patron saint of his home, La Palma island in the Canaries.

There are a number of cultural centres near the church. The **Centro Cultural Correios** ① *R Visconde de Itaboraí 20, T021-2253 1580, www.correios.com.br, Tue-Sun 1200-1900, free*, in a smart early 20th-century building with a little private park, is a good stop for an air-conditioned juice or coffee. It has a theatre, a 1000-sq-m concert hall and spaces for temporary exhibitions and cultural events, and a postage stamp fair on Saturdays. Just opposite, with entrances on Avenida Presidente Vargas and Rua 1 de Março 66, is the **Centro Cultural Banco do Brasil (CCBB)** ① *R 1 de Março 66, T021-3808 2020, www. bb.com.br/cultura, Tue-Sun 1000-2100*, in a fine early 19th-century neoclassical building with a beautiful glass domed roof. The centre hosts many of the city's large and distinguished art shows, including some excellent photographic exhibitions. It also has an arts cinema, library, multimedia facilities and lunchtime concerts (around US$5). The restaurant is air conditioned and the food respectable. At the corner of Rua Visconde de Itaboraí (No 253) and Avenida Presidente Vargas, just opposite Candelária, is the **Casa França-Brasil** ① *R Visconde de Itaboraí 78, T021-2253 5366, www.casafrancabrasil.com. br, Tue-Sun 1000-2000*, a Franco-Brazilian cultural centre designed by one of the key players in the 19th-century French cultural mission to Rio, Grandjean de Montigny. It holds temporary exhibitions exploring the long relationship between the two countries. The newest of the cultural centres near Candelária is the **Espaço Cultural da Marinha** ① *Av Alfredo Agache, on the waterfront, T021-2104 6025, www.sdm.mar.mil.br/espaco.htm, Tue-Sun 1200-1700, free*. This former naval establishment, built on a jetty over the bay, now contains museums of underwater archaeology and navigation. *Galeota*, the boat used by the Portuguese royal family for sailing around the Baía de Guanabara is kept here and a Second World War submarine and warship, the *Bauru* (not to be confused with the sandwich of the same name), is moored outside. The museum is very popular with Brazilian children and is crowded at weekends.

Just offshore, but connected to the mainland by a causeway to Ilha das Cobras, is the **Ilha Fiscal** ① *Av Alfredo Agache, T021-2233 9165, boats leave Thu-Sun at 1300, 1430 and 1600, closed 1 Jan, Carnaval, Holy Week and Christmas; when the sea is too rough transport is by van*. It was built as a customs house at the emperor's request, but he deemed it too beautiful, and said that it should be used only for official parties. Only one was ever held – a masked ball hosted by the viscount of Ouro Preto in honour of the crew of the Chilean warship, *The Admiral Cochrane*, five days before the republic began. It is now a museum, linked with the Espaço Cultural da Marinha. The island is passed by the ferry to Niterói.

Mosteiro de São Bento and Museu de Arte do Rio

The **Praça Mauá**, which lies north of Avenida Presidente Vargas, marks the end of Centro and the beginning of the port zone, which is being completely re-invented and revitalized in preparation for the 2016 Olympics, under the Porto Maravilha programme (www.portomaravilha.com.br – check the website for the latest openings). The myriad empty warehouses will be replaced by leisure areas, accommodation and a series of new museums and galleries. These include the **Museu de Arte do Rio (MAR)** ⓘ *Praça Mauá, T021-2203 1235, www.museumar.com, Tue-Fri 1000-1700, US$4*, the first of whose galleries opened in early 2013. The museum showcases artists responsible for the establishment of the Brazilian style (including Burle Marx, Castagneto, Dall'Ara, Di Cavalcanti, Facchinetti, Goeldi, Iberê Camargo, Ismael Nery and Lygia Clark) and those who are shaping Brazilian art today, through some of the city's most exciting temporary exhibitions, drawing on the relationship those artists have with Rio.

The sober Brazilian baroque façade of the **Mosteiro de São Bento** ⓘ *R Gerardo 68, T021-2516 2286, www.osb.org.br, daily 0700-1730, free, guided tours Mon-Sat 0900-1600; modest dress, no shorts; taxi from the city centre US$6*, sits nearby on a promontory looking out over the bay. It is widely publicized as a World Heritage Site, which it is not. But of all the city's colonial buildings this is the most worth visiting, both for its magnificent interior and for its significance as the most important Benedictine monument outside Europe. The church began life in 1586 with a group of monks who arrived in Rio from Salvador and it grew to become the most powerful monastery in the city. It preserves a lavish gilt baroque interior but is very poorly lit (the church charges an absurd US$5 to put on all of the electric lights). However, in the gloom it is possible to make out that not an inch remains unadorned. The three doors sculpted by Father Domingos da Conceição, which give access to the nave, and the sculptures of St Benedict, St Escolastica and Our Lady of Monserrat are particularly remarkable. The last, which is also by Domingos de Conceição, has painted birds' eggs for eyes. The painting is as wonderful as the carving; particularly the panels in the Blessed Sacrament chapel by Inácio Ferreira Pinto and *O Salvador*, the masterpiece of Brazil's first painter, Frei Ricardo do Pilar, which hangs in the sacristy. The enormous candelabra are attributed to Mestre Valentim, Rio's most celebrated church artisan, and are made from solid silver especially imported from Peru and the mines of Potosí in Bolivia at a price higher than Brazil's own gold. The monastery's library (open to men only) preserves a number of priceless religious manuscripts alongside 200,000 other books.

São Bento can be reached either by a narrow road from Rua Dom Gerardo 68, or by a lift whose entrance is at Rua Dom Gerardo 40. Both routes lead to a *praça* with tall trees. Arriving in the lift is more magical as you are whisked from the heat and bustle of the dock area to an oasis of calm, which sets the mood beautifully for a wander around the monastery buildings. If you would rather walk, the monastery is a few minutes from Praça Mauá, turning left off Avenida Rio Branco; Rua Dom Gerardo 68 is behind the massive new RBI building. Every Sunday at 1000 there is a Latin Mass with plainsong. Arrive an hour early to get a seat. On other days, Mass is at 0715 and the monks often sing at vespers.

Largo da Carioca and around

This higgledy-piggledy street of colonial churches, modern buildings and street stalls sits between Rua da Carioca and the Carioca *metrô* station about 1 km south of Praça XV along Rua da Assembléia. There is a variety of interesting sights here within a very small area. The **Convento de Santo Antônio** ① *T021-2262 0129, Mon, Wed, Thu, Fri 0730-1900, Tue 0630-2000, Sat 0730-1100 and 1530-1700, Sun 0900-1100, free*, the second oldest in Rio, sits on a little hill off the Largo da Carioca. You will often see single women here gathered to pray: there are many more women than men in Brazil and St Anthony is traditionally a provider of husbands. The church interior is baroque around the chancel, main altars and two lateral altars, which are devoted to St Anthony, St Francis and the Immaculate Conception respectively. The beautiful sacristy is decorated with *azulejos* (tiles) and adorned with paintings depicting scenes from St Anthony's life. Many members of the Brazilian imperial family are buried in the mausoleum. Separated from this church only by a fence of iron railings is one of Rio's least known and most beautiful baroque jewels: the little church of the **Ordem Terceira de São Francisco da Penitência** ① *T021-2262 0197, Mon-Fri 0900-1200 and 1300-1600, free*, which was built between 1622 and 1738. It has a splendid gilt interior by Francisco Xavier de Brito, who is largely credited with introducing baroque to Brazil and who was probably Aleijadinho's teacher in Ouro Preto. There's a also a fine panel depicting the glorification of St Francis by Caetano da Costa Coelho Behind the church is a tranquil catacomb-filled garden.

A couple of streets north, at the end of Rua do Ouvidor and dominating the square that bears its name, is the twin-towered **Igreja de São Francisco de Paula** ① *Largo São Francisco de Paula, Mon-Fri 0900-1300, free*, with some fine examples of Carioca art including carvings by Mestre Valentim, paintings by Vítor Meireles and murals by Manuel da Cunha. Across the Largo de São Francisco is the **Igreja de Nossa Senhora do Rosário e São Benedito dos Pretos** ① *on the corner of R Uruguaiana 77 and Ouvidor, T021-2224 2900, Mon-Fri 0700-1700, Sat 0700-1300, free*. Since the 17th century this church has been at the centre of African Christian culture in Rio. During the 19th century it was the site of an elaborate festival that recreated scenes from the courtly life of the king of Congo. A king and queen were crowned and they danced through the nearby streets followed by long parades of courtiers in fancy dress; a precursor perhaps for Carnaval. It was here that the announcements for the final abolition of slavery were prepared. The church once had a fabulous gilt interior but this was sadly destroyed in a fire in 1967. Next to the church is a small museum devoted to slavery in Brazil, whose collection of instruments of subjugation speaks starkly of life for black people in the last Western country to abolish the slave trade.

The **Real Gabinete Português de Leitura** ⓘ *R Luís Camões 30, T021-2221 3138, www.realgabinete.com.br, Mon-Fri 0900-1800, free*, sits just to the north of Largo São Francisco de Paula on Rua Luís de Camões. This is one of the city's hidden architectural treasures and one of the best pieces of mock-Manueline architecture in Brazil. Manueline architecture is usually described as Portuguese gothic and takes its name from King Manuel I who ruled Portugal between 1495 and 1521. It is unlike any other European gothic style, drawing strongly on Islamic and nautical themes – a lavish fusion of Islamic ornamentalism and sculpted seaweeds, anchors, ropes and corals, typified by the Cristo monastery in Tomar and the Mosteiro dos Jerônimos in Lisbon. The modest exterior of the Real Gabinete, which was designed by Portuguese architect Rafael da Silva e Castro in 1880, was inspired by the façade of Jerônimos. It is decorated with statues of Camões, Henry the Navigator, Vasco da Gama and Pedro Álvares Cabral, who claimed Brazil for Portugal. More interesting, however, is the magnificent reading hall built around the oldest central steel structure in Rio. Towering arches decorated with Islamic flourish ascend via coiled wooden ropes to an elaborate painted ceiling with skylights from which a massive iron chandelier is suspended. There are some 120,000 books in the library's collection, many of them very rare. The magnificent belle-époque coffee house, **Confeitaria Colombo**, is a short walk to the east, at Rua Gonçalves Dias 32 (see Restaurants, page 76).

Praça Tiradentes and the cathedral

One long block behind the Largo da Carioca and São Francisco de Paula is **Praça Tiradentes**, old and shady, with a **statue to Dom Pedro I** carved in 1862 by Luís Rochet. The emperor sits on horseback shouting his famous 1822 declaration of independence, the Grito de Ipiranga: 'Liberty or Death'. The **Teatro João Caetano** sits on the northeastern corner of the *praça* and is named after a famous 19th-century actor. Prince Dom Pedro first showed the green and yellow Brazilian flag in the original building, which was an important venue for meetings discussing Brazilian independence. The current theatre was constructed in 1920 after the original had fallen into disrepair. Two canvases by one of the city's most celebrated artists, Emiliano

Di Cavalcanti, hang on the second floor. Just north of the *praça*, in a handsome salmon pink colonial building, is the **Centro de Arte Hélio Oiticica** ⓘ *R Luís de Camões 68, Mon-Fri 1000-1800*, named after another famous Carioca artist and now a smart contemporary art exhibition space with six galleries, a good art bookshop and an air-conditioned café. Important national and international artists exhibit here. Shops in nearby streets specialize in selling goods for *umbanda*, the Afro-Brazilian religion. The **Catedral Metropolitana de São Sebastião** ⓘ *Av República do Chile, T021-2240 2669, www.catedral.com.br, daily 0700-1900, Mass Mon-Fri 1100, Sun 1000*, lies just south of the Praça Tiradentes and the Largo da Carioca; bordering Cinêlandia to the east and Lapa to the south. It is an oblate concrete cone fronted by a decorative ladder and replete with rich blue stained glass, which looks like a modernist Mayan temple. The design could be mistaken for a Niemeyer, but is in fact by another Brazilian Le Corbusier disciple, Edgar de Oliveira da Fonseca, with heavy modernist statues and panels by Humberto Cozzi. It's best to visit in the late afternoon when the sunlight streams through the immense monotone stained-glass windows. There is a small sacred art museum in the crypt, which has a handful of relics including Dom Pedro II's throne and the fonts used for the baptizing of imperial Brazilian babies. The *bonde* (tram) to Santa Teresa (due to re-open for 2014) leaves from behind the cathedral, the entrance is on Rua Senador Dantas (see page 47). Soon after leaving the station the tram traverses the Arcos da Lapa offering wonderful views.

One of the city's quirkier museums lies just a short walk from the cathedral. The **Museu de Farmácia Antônio Lago** ⓘ *R dos Andradas 96, 10th floor, T021-2263 0791, www.abf.org.br/index.php/museu, Mon-Fri 1430-1700 by appointment only via email abf@abf.org.br, US$2*, is a reproduction of a 17th-century Brazilian apothecary's shop, complete with Dr Jekyll cabinets and rows of dubious-looking herbal preparations in glass and porcelain vessels.

Cinelândia and Avenida Rio Branco

The area around Praça Floriano was the liveliest part of the city in the 1920s and 1930s when Hollywood hit Brazil. All of the best cinemas were situated here and their popularity became so great that the *praça* was named after them. Today **Cinelândia** remains lively, especially at the end of the week, owing to its proximity to the city's nightlife capital, Lapa. The 30-m-wide **Avenida Rio Branco**, which bisects Cinelândia, is the financial heart of the city. Lined by an untidy mishmash of modernist and art deco skyscrapers it was built at the turn of 20th the century under the 'tear it down' regime of Mayor Pereira Passos. Rio once had long stately avenues that rivalled the best of Buenos Aires but only clusters have survived. Although it has seen better days, the **Theatro Municipal** ⓘ *Praça Floriano, T021-2332 9191, www.theatromunicipal.rj.gov. br, Mon-Fri 1300-1700, bilingual guided tours by appointment T021-2299 1667,* remains a splendid piece of French-inspired, lavish neoclassical pomp. The tour is worth it to see front of house and backstage, the decorations and the machine rooms – a luxuriously ornate temple to an early 20th-century Carioca high society. On either side of the ostentatious colonnaded façade are rotundas, surmounted by cupolas. The muses of poetry and music watch over all, alongside an imperial eagle, wings outstretched and poised for flight. The interior is a mock-European fantasy of Carrara-marble columns, crystal chandeliers and gilt ceilings fronted by a vast sweeping, *Gone With the Wind* staircase. The stage is one of the largest in the world. The theatre was designed by Francisco de Oliveira Passos, son of the contemporaneous city mayor, who won an ostensibly open architectural competition together with French architect Albert Guilbert.

Opposite, on the other side of Avenida Rio Branco, is the refurbished **Museu Nacional de Belas-Artes** ① *Av Rio Branco 199, T021-2219 8474, www.mnba. gov.br, Tue-Fri 1000-1800, Sat and Sun 1200-1700, US$4, free on Sun.* Fine art in Rio and in Brazil was, as a whole, stimulated by the arrival in 1808 of the Portuguese royal family. In 1816 the Academia de Belas-Artes was founded by another Frenchman, Joaquim Lebreton. This building was constructed 1906-1908 to house the national gallery and contains the best collection of art in the country. This includes depictions of Brazil by European visitors such as Dutchman Frans Post and Frenchman Jean-Baptiste Debret, and the best of 20th-century Brazilian art by important names such as modernist and social realist Cândido Portinari, Emiliano Di Cavalcanti (famous for his iconographic images of black Cariocas at a time when racism was institutionalized in Rio), Tarsila do Amaral (founder of the first major school of Brazilian Art, *antropofagismo*, which strongly influenced *tropicália*) and the brutalist art deco sculptor Victor Brecheret. Another gallery contains further works by foreign artists and the temporary exhibition hall houses many of Rio de Janeiro's most important international exhibitions.

Another of Cinelândia's stately neoclassical buildings is the **Biblioteca Nacional** ① *Av Rio Branco 219/239, T021-3095 3879, www.bn.br, Mon-Fri 0900-2000, Sat 0900-1500, free,* an eclectic Carioca construction, this time with a touch of art nouveau. The library is fronted by a stately engaged portico supported by a Corinthian colonnade. Inside is a series of monumental staircases in Carrara marble. The stained glass in the windows is French. The first national library was brought to Brazil in 1808 by the Prince Regent, Dom João, from a collection in the Ajuda Palace in Lisbon. Today the library houses more than nine million items, including a first edition of the *Lusiad of Camões*, a 15th-century Moguncia Bible and Book of Hours, paintings donated by Pedro II, scores by Mozart and etchings by Dürer.

Nearby, in the former Ministry of Education and Health building, is the **Palácio Gustavo Capanema** ① *R da Imprensa 16, off the Esplanada do Castelo,* at the junction of Av Graça Aranha and R Araújo Porto Alegre, just off Av Rio Branco, T021-2220 1490, by appointment only, Mon-Fri 0900-1800. Dating back to 1937-1945, it was the first piece of modernist architecture in the Americas and was designed by an illustrious team of architects led by Lúcio Costa (under the guidance of Le Corbusier) and included a very young Oscar Niemeyer – working on his first project. Inside are impressive murals by Cândido Portinari, one of Brazil's most famous artists, as well as works by other well-known names. The gardens were laid out by Roberto Burle Marx who was responsible for many landscaping projects throughout Rio (including the Parque do Flamengo) and who worked with Costa and Niemeyer in Brasília.

Lapa → *See map, page 48.*

Only a decade ago Lapa, which lies just south of the cathedral on the edge of Cinelândia, was a no-go area; tawdry and terrifying, walked only by prostitutes, thugs and drug addicts chasing the dragon in the crumbling porticoes of the early 20th-century and art nouveau buildings. The area can still feel a little edgy, especially on weekdays after dark. But it has undergone an unimagined renaissance. This was once the Montmartre of Rio; the painter Di Cavalcanti wrote poetically of wandering its streets at night on his way home to Flamengo, past the little cafés and ballrooms and the rows of handsome townhouses. Now the cafés are alive once more, spilling out onto the streets, and the ballrooms and townhouses throb with samba and electronica. Opera is once more performed in the concert halls of the Escola de Música, and the area's once notorious thoroughfare, Rua do Lavradio, is now lined with smart little restaurants and clubs, playing host to one of the city's most interesting bric-a-brac and antiques markets on Saturdays. → *See Bars and clubs, page 80.*

Although the area is best seen on a cautious wander after 2100 at the end of the week, or during the Rua do Lavradio market (which takes place on the first Saturday of every month), there are a few interesting sights. The most photographed are the **Arcos da Lapa**, built in 1744 as an aqueduct to carry water from Santa Teresa to the Chafariz da Carioca, with its 16 drinking fountains, in the centre of the city. The aqueduct's use was changed at the end of the 19th century, with the introduction of electric trams in Rio. Tracks were laid on top of the arches and the inaugural run was on 1 September 1896 for a tramline, one of the city's most delightful journeys; running from behind the Catedral de São Sebastião to Santa Teresa (due to re-open 2014).

Bars huddle under their southern extremity on Avenida Mem de Sá, one of Rio's most popular nightlife streets. Street performers (and vagrants) often gather in the cobbled square between the *arcos* and the cathedral. There are a number of moderately interesting buildings off this square. The eclectic baroque/neoclassical **Escola da Musica da Universidade Federal do Rio de Janeiro** ⓘ *R do Passeio 98, only officially open for performances*, has one of the city's best concert halls. A stroll away is the bizarre baroque façade of another prestigious classical concert hall, the **Sala Cecília Mereilles** ⓘ *Largo da Lapa 47*. More picturesque are the mosaic-tiled **Ladeira do Santa Teresa** stairs, which wind their way steeply from the square and from the back of Rua Teotônio to Santa Teresa. These are much beloved of music video directors and fashion photographers who use them as a backdrop to carefully produced gritty urban scenes. The steps are tiled in red, gold and green and bordered by little houses, many of which are dishevelled and disreputable but wonderfully picturesque. Be vigilant here.

North of Avenida Mem de Sá is **Rua do Lavradio**. This was one of urban Rio's first residential streets and is lined with handsome 18th- and early 20th-century townhouses. These are now filled with samba clubs, cafés, bars and antiques shops. Any day is good for a browse and a wander, and on Saturdays at the end of the month there is a busy antiques market, live street tango, no cars and throngs of people from all sections of Carioca society. Some of the houses here were once grand. Number 84 once belonged to the marquis who gave the street its name. Further along is what was once Brazil's foremost Masonic lodge, the imposing **Palácio Maçônico Grande Oriente do Brasil**, which tellingly has had as its grand masters King Dom Pedro I and one of the country's most important republican politicians, José Bonifácio Andrada e Silva.

Central do Brasil railway station
Central do Brasil or **Dom Pedro II** railway station, as it is also known, once served much of the country but now serves only Rio. This brutal 1930s art deco temple to progress was one of the city's first modernist buildings and was made famous by the Walter Salles film *Central do Brasil* (Central Station). The film's thronging crowd scenes were set here. For similar shots come with your camera in the morning or evening and watch hundreds of thousands of people bustle in and out of trains leaving for the northern and western parts of Rio.

Gamboa, Cidade Nova and the Sambódromo
In the early 20th century, after the Paraguayan war and the abolition of slavery but before the warehouses were built in **Gamboa**, this northern dockland area was known as 'Little Africa' due to the high number of resident Bahian immigrants. With them, the African-Bahian rhythms of the *candomblé* religion were introduced into the Carioca community and the next generation spawned a host of famous local musicians that included Donga, Chico da Baiana and João de Baiana.

The streets and back yards of Gamboa became the birthplace of a new music: samba, born of Angolan *semba* rhythms fused with European singing styles and instruments. Donga and João da Baiana used to gather on the Pedra do Sal stairs close to the Praça Mauá to play and hold impromptu music and samba dance parties. Later the dance was incorporated into an alternative Mardi Gras festival as a counterpart to the ballroom dances of the white elite. Street parade clubs were formed by another young Carioca, Hilário Jovino Ferreira. Their structure was copied later by the much larger samba schools that still produce the Carnaval parades today.

In 2008 the city government inaugurated the **Cidade do Samba (Samba City)** ① *R Rivadávia Corréa 60, Gamboa, T021-2213 2503, http:// cidadedosambarj.globo.com, Tue-Sat 1000-1900*, both to celebrate samba and to bring the administrative and production houses of the samba schools under one roof. The famous samba schools from the **Liga Independente das Escolas de Samba (LIESA)** now have a permanent carnival production centre of 14 workshops, each of them housed in a two-storey building. Visitors can watch floats and costumes being prepared or watch one of the year-round carnival-themed shows. A visit here is a wonderful experience and a real eye-opener, offering the chance to see how much painstaking work goes into creating the floats, costumes and dances of schools such as the **Primeira Estação de Mangueira** (see page 86), for one night of lavish display. Rio's carnival is nailed, glued, stitched and sewn over an entire year. Much of the work is undertaken by **AMEBRAS** ① *www.amebras.org.br*, an association of stern older women who enrol, train and employ dozens of would-be artisans and dressmakers from the *favelas*. Thus carnival is an industry that revitalizes poor Rio. In the words of AMEBRAS president Célia Regina Domingues "there's no fooling about here – everything we do, from hat-making to foam-sculpting for the floats, is directed towards a profession, post-carnival. People leave our project with real skills." There is a gift shop at the Cidade do Samba where it is possible to buy Carnaval costumes and souvenirs, many by AMEBRAS, or you can request a visit through their website as part of a visit to the Cidade. The Cidade do Samba has weekly samba shows, tickets for which can be purchased at the booths near the main entrance.

Carnaval happens right next to Gamboa in the **Cidade Nova**. Oscar Niemeyer's 650-m stadium street, the **Sambódromo** ① *R Marquês de Sapucaí s/n, Metrô Central or Metrô Praça Onze, Cidade Nova, T021-2502 6996, Mon-Fri 0900-1700*, was purpose-built for the annual parades and is well-worth a visit at any time. ➤➤ *See box, page 88.*

Near the Sambódromo, in the Boca do Lixo, is the **Crescer and Viver Circus** ① *R Boca do Lixo, Thu-Sat from Aug to late Nov, tours are available, see www. crescereviver.org.br; Metrô Praça Onze, but do not walk in this neighbourhood – come by cab*, another of Rio's inspiring community projects. "If it weren't for our circus", says Vinícius Daumas of Projeto Crescer and Viver, "I can honestly say that many of these teenagers would be dead. For sure some would be in a trafficking gang." Instead, some 2000 kids from the deprived communities of the Boca do Lixo neighbourhood have gone to circus school and learnt their three Rs whilst also mastering the trapeze and the flic-flac. The company performs a spectacular show to music composed by Luíz Gonzaga's grandson, Daniel, in a tent in the Boca do Lixo. The circus was closed in early 2013 but has plans to recommence before the 2014 FIFA World Cup™. Check the website for details.

Nearby, **Praça Onze** is today the terminus of the city's main thoroughfare, Avenida Presidente Vargas. But it was once a square and an established meeting place for *capoeristas* whose acrobatic martial art to the rhythm of the *berimbau* and hand clap inspired much Carnaval choreography. A replica of the head of a Nigerian prince from the British Museum, erected in honour of **Zumbi dos Palmares**, sits on Avenida Presidente Vargas itself. Zumbi was a Bantu prince who became the most successful black slave emancipator in the history of the Americas, founding a kingdom within Brazil in the 19th century. The **Centro de Memória do Carnaval** ① *Av Rio Branco 4, 2nd floor, T021-3213 5151, www.liesa.globo.com, visits by appointment only*, is a research centre and preserves one of the largest repositories of international and Brazilian carnival images, documents and publications in the world.

Northern Rio → *For listings, see pages 70-103.*

Nossa Senhora da Penha
① *Largo da Penha 19, T021-2290 0942, www.santuariodapenhario.com.br, Tue-Sun 1000-1600.*
The church of Nossa Senhora da Penha, is one of the most important pilgrimage centres in the whole country, especially for black Brazilians. It sits on an enormous rock, into whose side 365 steps have been carved. Pilgrims ascend these on their knees during the festival month of October. The church in its present form dates from the early 20th century, but it was modelled on an early 18th-century chapel and a religious building has been on this site since the original hermitage was built in 1632. There are great views from the summit.

To get there take the *metrô* to Del Castilho. Leave the station to the left, walk down the passageway and catch microbus (*micro-ônibus*) No 623 labelled 'Penha-Shopping Nova América 2' to the last stop. Get off at the shopping centre, in front of Rua dos Romeiros, and walk up that street to the Largo da Penha from where there are signposts to the church.

Maracanã stadium
① *Av Prof Eurico Rabelo, T021-2334 1705, www.maracanaonline.com.br, daily 0900-1700; independent visit Gate 15, guided tours of the newly renovated stadium due to recommence in late 2013 from Gate 16 (in Portuguese or English, daily 0930-1700, US$10). Take the* metrô *to Maracanã station on Linha 2, one stop beyond São*

Cristóvão. Bus Nos 238 and 239 from the centre, 434 and 464 from Glória, Flamengo and Botafogo, 455 from Copacabana, and 433 and 464 from Ipanema and Leblon all go to the stadium. Trips to football matches can be organized through www. bealocal.com. It is not advisable to drive in this part of Rio.

Whilst tour guides proclaim Maracanã the largest sports stadium in the world, in fact there are several larger stadiums, including Indianapolis in the USA and Strahov stadium in Prague. But Maracanã was the largest when it was first built and remains impressive – not least because it is the hallowed temple to the most important religious practice in Brazil: the worship of football. This is where Pelé scored his 1000th goal in 1969. His feet, as well as those of Ronaldo and other Brazilian stars, are immortalized in concrete outside the stadium. The stadium hosted the largest crowd ever to see a football match in 1950 when Brazil lost to Uruguay in front of about 200,000 spectators – an event that shook the national psyche and which is known as the Maracanazo tragedy.

In 2012-2013, Maracanã was completely rebuilt and refurbished for the 2014 FIFA World Cup™, shrinking to some 80,000 seats. The project has been controversial, for whilst modest in its aims, it is expected to have cost an astounding US$400 million and includes the construction of 14,000 new parking spaces, 3000 of which are allocated inside Quinta da Boa Vista park.

Even if you're not a football fan, matches are worth going to for the spectators' samba bands and the adrenalin-charged atmosphere – try to catch a local or Rio-São Paulo derby, or an international game. There are four types of ticket: *Cadeira Especial* (special seats), the most expensive; *Arquibancada Branca* (white terraces), which give a good side view of the game; *Arquibancada Verde e Amarela* (green and yellow terraces), with a view from behind the goal; and *Cadeira Comum*. Prices vary according to the game, but it's more expensive to buy tickets from agencies than at the gate or via the internet; it is cheaper to buy tickets from club sites on the day before the match.

Don't take valuables or wear a watch and take special care when entering and leaving the stadium. The rivalry between the local clubs Flamengo and Vasco da Gama is intense, often leading to violence, so it is advisable to avoid their encounters. If you buy a club shirt, don't be tempted to wear it on match day: if you find yourself in the wrong place, you could be in trouble.

Quinta da Boa Vista

ⓘ *Take the* metrô *to São Cristóvão and follow signs to Quinta da Boa Vista, a 5-min walk. Beware of muggings on weekdays; don't take valuables.*

About 3 km west of Praça da República (beyond the Sambódromo) is the Quinta da Boa Vista, the emperor's private park from 1809 to 1889. The **Museu Nacional** ⓘ *T021-2562 6900, www.museunacional.ufrj.br, Tue-Sun 1000-1600, US$1.50*, is housed in the former imperial palace. The building is crumbling and the collections dusty and poorly displayed. Only the unfurnished throne room and ambassadorial reception room on the second floor reflect past glories. In the entrance hall is the famous Bendegó meteorite, found in the state of Bahia in 1888; its original weight, before some of it was chipped, was 5360 kg. Besides several collections of foreign pieces (including Peruvian and Mexican archaeology, Graeco-Roman ceramics and Egyptian mummies), the museum contains collections of Brazilian indigenous weapons, costumes, utensils and historical documents. There are also frowsty collections of stuffed birds, beasts, fish and butterflies.

Also in the park is the **Jardim Zoológico** ① *Av Dom Pedro II, T021-3878 4200, Tue-Sun 0900-1630, US$3, young children free, students with ID half-price.* The zoo is in the northeastern corner of the park. It has a collection of 2100 animals, most of which are kept in modern, spacious enclosures, and there is an important captive breeding programme for golden-headed and golden lion tamarins, spectacled bears and yellow-throated capuchin monkeys. The aviary is impressive and children can enjoy a ride in a little train through the park.

Santa Teresa → *For listings, see pages 70-103.*

A bus or tram ride from Rio's centre or Guanabara Bay suburbs to Santa Teresa is a magical experience – winding up the hilly streets lined with pretty colonial houses and lavish mansions towards the forested slopes of Tijuca National Park, and leaving sweeping views of Guanabara Bay and the Sugar Loaf in your wake. As you reach the summit of Morro do Desterro hill, where Santa Teresa lies, you pass the **Largo do Guimarães** and the **Largo das Neves**, little *praças* of shops and restaurants that feel as if they belong clustered around a village green rather than in a large city. Indeed Santa Teresa feels almost like a town in itself rather than a neighbourhood, with a strong community identity forged by one of the highest concentrations of artists, writers and musicians in the city. They congregate in bars like **O Mineiro**, on the Largo do Guimarães, **Bar Gomes** and **Bar Porto das Neves**, on the Largo das Neves. At weekends the lively nightlife spills over into clubs like **Espírito Santa** (see page 81) and then into neighbouring Lapa which is only a five-minute taxi ride away.

A sense of separation is reflected not only in the suburb's geography, but also its history. In 1624, Antônio Gomes do Desterro chose the area both for its proximity to Rio and its isolation, and erected a hermitage dedicated to Nossa Senhora do Desterro. The name was changed from Morro do Desterro to Santa Teresa after the construction in 1750 of a convent of that name dedicated to the patroness of the order. The convent exists to this day, but it can only be seen from the outside.

Arriving in Santa Teresa

Getting there and around Bus Nos 434 and 464 run from Leblon (via Ipanema, Copacabana and the Guanabara Bay suburbs to Avenida Riachuelo

4 Glória, Santa Teresa & Lapa

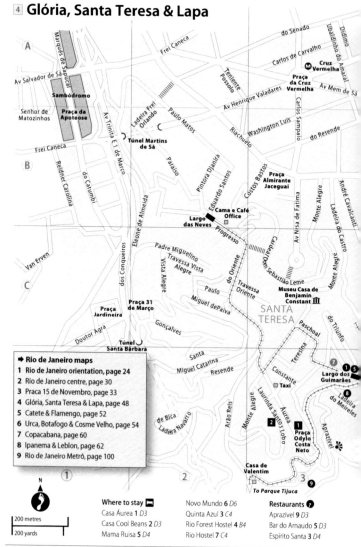

N

200 metres
200 yards

Where to stay 🛏
Casa Áurea 1 *D3*
Casa Cool Beans 2 *D3*
Mama Ruisa 5 *D4*

Novo Mundo 6 *D6*
Quinta Azul 3 *C4*
Rio Forest Hostel 4 *B4*
Rio Hostel 7 *C4*

Restaurants 🍴
Aprazível 9 *D3*
Bar do Arnaudo 5 *D3*
Espírito Santa 3 *D4*

in Lapa, a few hundred metres north of the arches) from where minibus No 014 Castelo (US$1.40) runs to the Largo do Guimarães. Taxis from Glória metrô to Santa Teresa cost around US$5. The famous yellow Santa Teresa trams are

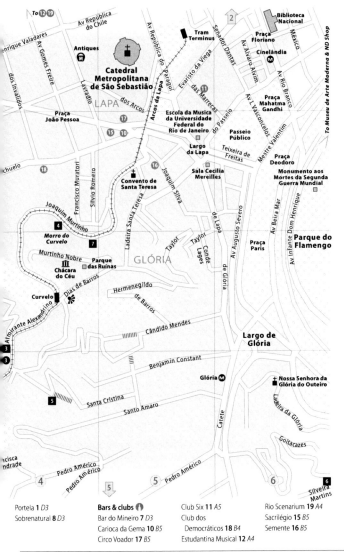

currently not running following a serious accident in 2011. They are due to start running again in time for the Olympics. The route runs from the Largo da Carioca, near the *metrô* station and the cathedral, passing over the Lapa viaduct and running along all the main streets in Santa Teresa (via the Largo do Guimarães and Largo das Neves), eventually reaching either Dois Irmãos or Paula Mattos at the far end of Santa Teresa (see page 47).

In recent years, Santa Teresa has had a reputation for crime, however, the area is much more heavily policed nowadays and you should encounter few problems. Nonetheless it's best to be vigilant with your camera at all times, and be particularly wary after dark. Steer clear of any steps that lead down the hill, on and around Rua Almirante Alexandrino or at the Tijuca end of Largo dos Guimarães.

Places in Santa Teresa

Santa Teresa is best explored on foot: wander the streets to admire the colonial buildings or stop for a beer in a little streetside café and marvel at the view. The better colonial houses, most of which are private residences, include the **Casa de Valentim** (a castle-like house in Vista Alegre), the tiled **Chácara dos Viegas**, in Rua Monte Alegre, and the **Chalé Murtinho**. The latter was the house in which Dona Laurinda Santos Lobo held her famous artistic, political and intellectual salons at the turn of the 20th century. The house was in ruins until it was partially restored and turned into a cultural centre called **Parque das Ruínas** ① *R Murtinho Nobre 41, daily 1000-1700*. It has superb views of the city, an exhibition space and an open-air stage (live music on Thursday). Next door is the **Chácara do Céu**, or **Museu Castro Maya** ① *R Murtinho Nobre 93, T021-3970 1126, www.museuscastromaya.com.br, Wed-Mon 1200-1700, US$1*, housed in the former home of the Carioca millionaire and art collector, Raymundo Ottoni de Castro Maya. It has a wide range of works by modern painters, including Modigliani and important Brazilian artists such as Di Cavalacanti. There are wonderful views out over Guanabara Bay. There are also superb views from the **Museu Casa de Benjamin Constant** ① *R Monte Alegre 225, T021-2509 1248, Wed-Sun 1300-1700*, the former home of the Carioca military engineer and positivist philosopher who helped to found the Republic.

Glória, Catete and Flamengo → *For listings, see pages 70-103.*

The city centre is separated from Copacabana and the other ocean beaches by a series of long white-sand coves that fringe Guanabara Bay and which are divided by towering rocks. The first of the coves is the **Enseada da Glória**, fronting the suburb of the same name and sitting next to the Santos Dumont Airport. Avenida Infante Dom Henrique, a broad avenue lined with an eclectic mix of grand houses and squat office blocks, leads from here to what was once the city's finest beach, **Flamengo**, a long stretch of sand separated from the rest of southern Rio by the Morro da Viúva (widow's peak). The suburb of **Catete** lies just behind Flamengo. These three areas were once the heart of recreational Rio; the posing-spots of choice for the belle-époque middle and upper classes and perhaps the most coveted urban beaches in the world. These days the water is polluted and swimming ill-advised, but the suburbs are pleasant for a stroll.

Arriving in Glória, Catete and Flamengo
Bus No 119 from the centre or No 571 from Copacabana serve the neighbourhoods, as does the *metrô*. The centrepiece of the three suburbs are the gardens of the Parque do Flamengo, on Avenida Infante Dom Henrique, reached from Metrô Glória, Catete, Largo de Machado or Flamengo.

Places in Glória, Catete and Flamengo
Before the pollution became too much, Burle Marx, Brazil's 20th-century Capability Brown, designed the **Parque do Flamengo**, a handsome stretch of waterfront to separate Avenida Infante Dom Henrique from the city's most glorious beach, and gave it ample shade with a range of tropical trees and stands of stately royal palms. The gardens stretch from Glória through to the Morro da Viúva at the far end of Flamengo; they were built on reclaimed land and opened in 1965 to mark the 400th anniversary of the city's founding. The lawns and promenade are favourite spots for smooching lovers, especially at sundown. There are children's play areas and a handful of monuments and museums. These include the impressive postmodern **Monumento aos Mortos da Segunda Guerra Mundial** ① *Av Infante Dom Henrique, Tue-Sun 1000-1700 for the crypt museum; beach clothes and flip flops not permitted*, the national war memorial to Brazil's dead in the Second World War. The gently curved slab is supported by two slender columns, representing two palms uplifted to heaven and guarded by soldiers from the adjacent barracks. In the crypt are the remains of the Brazilian soldiers killed in Italy in 1944-1945. At the far northern end of the Parque do Flamengo is the **Museu de Arte Moderna** ① *Av Infante Dom Henrique 85, T021-2240 4944, www.mamrio.com.br, Tue-Fri 1200-1800, last entry 1730, Sat and Sun 1200-1900, last entry 1830, US$6*, another striking modernist building with the best collection of modern art in Brazil outside São Paulo. Works by many well-known Europeans sit alongside collections of Brazilian modern and contemporary art including drawings by Cândido Portinari and etchings of everyday work scenes by Gregório Gruber.

The beautiful little church on the Glória hill, overlooking the Parque do Flamengo, is **Nossa Senhora da Glória do Outeiro** ① *T021-2225 2869, Tue-Fri 0900-1200 and 1300-1700, Sat and Sun 0900-1200, guided tours by appointment* *on the 1st Sun of each month*. Built 1735-1791, it was the favourite church of the imperial family and Dom Pedro II was baptized here. The building is polygonal, with a single tower. It contains some excellent examples of the best *azulejos* (tiles) in Rio and its main wooden altar was carved by Mestre Valentim. Next door is the small **Museum of Religious Art** ⓘ *T021-2556 6434, same hours as the church.*

Behind Glória and Flamengo is the rather down-at-heel suburb of Catete, which is dotted with museums. The best of these is the **Museu da República** ⓘ *R do Catete 153, T021-3235 2650, www.museudarepublica.org.br, Tue-Fri 1000-1700, Sat, Sun and holidays 1400-1800, US$4, free Wed and Sun, under 10s and over 65s free, half-price for students with ID*, the former palace of a coffee baron, the Barão de Nova Friburgo. The palace was built 1858-1866 and, in 1887, it was converted into the presidential seat, until the move to Brasília. The ground floor of this museum consists of the sumptuous rooms of the coffee baron's mansion. The first floor is devoted to the history of the Brazilian republic. You can also see the room where former president Getúlio Vargas shot himself. Behind the museum is the **Parque do Catete**, which contains many birds and monkeys and is a popular place for practising Tai Chi.

The **Museu do Folclore Edison Carneiro** ⓘ *R do Catete 181, T021-2285 0441, Tue-Fri 1100-1800, Sat and Sun 1500-1800, free*, houses a collection of amusing

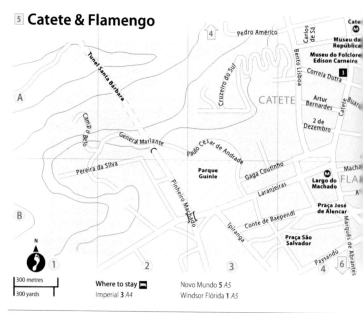

5 Catete & Flamengo

Where to stay 🛏
Imperial 3 *A4*

Novo Mundo 5 *A5*
Windsor Flórida 1 *A5*

but poorly labelled small ceramic figures representing everyday life in Brazil, some of which are animated by electric motors. Many artists are represented and displays show the way of life in different parts of the country. There are also fine *candomblé* and *umbanda* costumes, religious objects, displays about Brazil's festivals and a small but excellent library, with helpful staff who can help find books on Brazilian culture, history and anthropology. Flash photography is prohibited.

The **Museu Carmen Miranda** ① *Parque Brigadeiro Eduardo Gomes (Parque do Flamengo), Flamengo, T021-2334 4293, Tue-Fri 1100-1700, Sat and Sun 1300-1700, US$1,* has more than 3000 items related to the famous Portuguese singer forever associated with Rio, who emigrated to Brazil as a child and then moved to Hollywood. The collection includes some of her famous gowns, fruit-covered hats, jewellery and recordings. There are occasional showings of her films.

Botafogo, Urca and Pão de Açúcar (Sugar Loaf) → *For listings, see pages 70-103.*

Pão de Açúcar, or the **Sugar Loaf**, looms over the perfect wine-glass bay of **Botafogo**, the next cove after Flamengo. Huddled around the boulder's flanks is the suburb of **Urca**, home to a military barracks and the safest middle-class houses in Rio. Remnant forest, still home to marmosets and rare birds, shrouds the boulder's sides and a cable car straddles the distance between its summit, the **Morro de Urca** hill and the houses below, making one of the continent's most breathtaking views easily accessible. Urca and Botafogo have a few sights of interest and make convenient bases with decent accommodation and restaurant options, particularly in the lower price ranges.

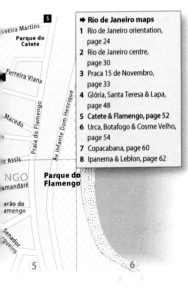

➔ **Rio de Janeiro maps**
1 Rio de Janeiro orientation, page 24
2 Rio de Janeiro centre, page 30
3 Praca 15 de Novembro, page 33
4 Glória, Santa Teresa & Lapa, page 48
5 Catete & Flamengo, page 52
6 Urca, Botafogo & Cosme Velho, page 54
7 Copacabana, page 60
8 Ipanema & Leblon, page 62

Arriving in Botafogo, Urca and Pão de Açúcar (Sugar Loaf)
Botafogo has a *metrô* station. Buses that run between Copacabana and the centre stop in Botafogo, so take any bus marked 'Centro' from

Copacabana or 'Copacabana' from the centre. Bus No 107 (from the centre, Catete or Flamengo) and No 511 from Copacabana (No 512 to return) take you to Urca; the cable car for the Sugar Loaf is on Praça General Tiburcio, next to the Rio de Janeiro federal university. The rides themselves go up in two stages, the first to the summit of Morro da Urca, the smaller rock that sits in front of the Sugar Loaf, and the second from there to the top of the Sugar Loaf itself. Allow at least two hours for your visit.

Pão de Açúcar (Sugar Loaf)

The western hemisphere's most famous monolith rises almost sheer from the dark sea to just under 400 m, towering over Botafogo beach and separating Guanabara Bay from the Atlantic Ocean. The views from the top, out over Copacabana, Ipanema and the mountains and forests of Corcovado and Tijuca,

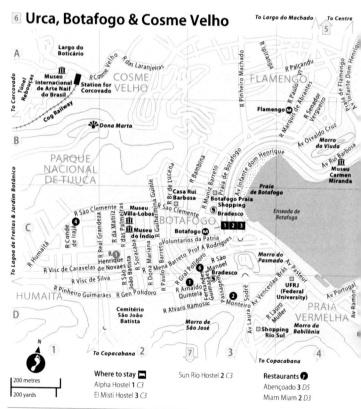

6 **Urca, Botafogo & Cosme Velho**

Where to stay 🛏
Alpha Hostel **1** C3
El Misti Hostel **3** C3

Sun Rio Hostel **2** C3

Restaurants 🍴
Abençoado **3** D5
Miam Miam **2** D3

are as unforgettable as the view from New York's Empire State Building or Victoria Peak in Hong Kong. The **cable car** ① *Av Pasteur 520, Praia Vermelha, Urca, T021-2461 2700, www.bondinho.com.br, daily 0800-1950, US$21 return, under 6s free, children 6-12 half-price, every 30 mins*, runs to the top where there are extensive paths, plentiful shade and snack bars. Come early for the clearest air, best views and smallest crowds.

Paths up and around the Sugar Loaf There is more to the Sugar Loaf than the views from the top. The surrounding rocks hide secluded little beaches, remnant forest and small colonial suburbs well worth exploring. The best place to begin is at **Praia Vermelha**, the beach to the south of the rock where there is a simple restaurant, the **Círculo Militar da Praia Vermelha** (no sign) with wonderful views. The paved walking track, **Pista Cláudio Coutinho** ① *daily 0700-1800*, runs from here along the waterfront around the foot of the rock. You'll see plenty of wildlife at dawn, especially marmosets and tanagers, along with various intrepid climbers scaling the granite. About 350 m from the beginning of the Pista Coutinho is a turning to the left for a path that winds its way up through the forest to the top of Morro de Urca, from where the cable car can be taken for US$7. You can save even more money by climbing the **Caminho da Costa**, a path to the summit of the Pão de Açúcar. Only one stretch of 10 m requires climbing gear; wait at the bottom of the path for a group going up. You can then descend to Morro de Urca by cable car for free and walk the rest of the way down. There are 35 rock-climbing routes up the boulder. The best months for climbing are April to August. ►► *See What to do, page 94.*

Botafogo

The Funai-run **Museu do Índio** ① *R das Palmeiras 55, T021-3214 8702, www. museudoindio.org.br, Mon-Fri 0900-1730, Sat and Sun 1300-1700, US$2.50,*

Oui Oui **4** *C1*
Raajmahal **6** *C3*
Yorubá **1** *D3*

Bars & clubs 🍸
Casa de Matriz **1** *C2*

free on Sun, 10-min walk from Botafogo metrô or bus No 571 from Catete, preserves some 12,000 objects from more than 180 Brazilian indigenous groups, including basketry, ceramics, masks and weapons as well as 500,000 documents and 50,000 photographs. Very few are on display and the museum's few rooms are mostly devoted to information panels and short film shows. The garden includes a Guaraní *maloca* and there is a small, well-displayed handicraft shop and a library of ethnology.

The **Museu Villa-Lobos** ① *R Sorocaba 200, T021-2266 3845, www. museuvillalobos. org.br, Mon-Fri 1000-1700, free, lunchtime concert US$6-17*, is a block east of the Museu do Índio. Such was the fame and respect afforded to Latin America's most celebrated composer that the museum was founded just one year after his death in 1960. Inside the fine 19th-century building is a collection of his personal objects including instruments, scores, books and recordings. The museum has occasional concerts and temporary shows and supports a number of classical music projects throughout Brazil.

The **Dona Marta viewpoint**, which sits in the forest immediately above Botafogo and is connected by road to Corcovado, offers the best views of the Sugar Loaf in the city. Do not visit after dusk as robbers from the nearby *favelas* frequent the roads.

Christ statue at Corcovado and Cosme Velho → *For listings, see pages 70-103.*

Few famous sights in the world live up to the high expectations overexposure has placed on them. The view from **Corcovado** mountain is one of them (see opposite page for opening hours and transport details). It is particularly impressive at dusk. Almost 1 km above the city and at the apex of one of the highest pinnacles in Tijuca forest stands **O Redentor** (Christ the Redeemer) lit in brilliant xenon and with arms open to embrace the urban world's most breathtaking view. At his feet to the west are a panoply of bays, fringed with white and backed by twinkling skyscrapers and the neon of myriad street lights. To the east as far as the eye can see lie long stretches of sand washed by green and white surf. In front and to the south, next to the vast ocean beaches, is the sparkle of Niterói watched over by low grey mountains and connected to Rio by a 10-km-long sinuous bridge that threads its way across the 10-km expanse of Guanabara Bay. As the light fades, the tropical forest at Christ's back comes to life in a chorus of cicadas and evening birdsong loud enough to drown even the chatter of 1000 tourists.

At the base of the mountain is the sleepy suburb of **Cosme Velho**, leafy and dotted with grand houses, museums and a little artist's corner called the Largo do Boticario. The two are linked by a 3.8-km railway, opened in 1884 by Emperor Dom Pedro II.

Arriving in Corcovado and Cosme Velho

There are several ways to reach the top of Corcovado. The Trem do Corcovado cog railway and a road connect the city to the mountain from the suburb of Cosme Velho. Both are on the northern side of the Rebouças tunnel, which runs to and from the Lagoa. From the upper terminus of the **cog railway** ⓘ *R Cosme Velho 513, T021-2558 1329, www.corcovado.com.br, daily every 30 mins 0830-1830, 15 min-journey, US$12 one-way, US$22 return, come early to avoid long queues,* there is a climb of 220 steps to the top or you can take the newly installed escalator, near which there is a café. Mass is held on Sunday in a small chapel in the statue pedestal. There is a museum at the station with panels showing the history of the statue and the railway. To get to the cog railway station take a taxi or bus to Cosme Velho and get off at the station.

Buses are as follows: from the centre or Glória/Flamengo bus No 180; from Copacabana bus Nos 583 or 584; from Botafogo or Ipanema/Leblon bus Nos 583 or 584; from Santa Teresa take the *micro-ônibus*.

Taxis, which wait in front of the station, also offer tours of Corcovado and Mirante Dona Marta and cost around US$25.

If going **on foot**, take bus No 206 from Praça Tiradentes (or No 407 from Largo do Machado) to Silvestre, where there is a station at which the train no longer stops. It is a steep 9-km walk from here to the top, along a shady road. Take the narrow street to the right of the station, go through the gate used by people who live beside the tracks and continue to the national park entrance. Walkers are charged entrance fees, even if you walk all the way you still have to pay for the van – it is an illegal charge, but in a country with as high a level of corruption as Brazil they can get away with it. Allow a minimum of two hours (up to four hours depending on fitness).

By **car**, drive through Túnel Rebouças from Lagoa and then look out for the Corcovado signs before the beginning of the second tunnel and off to your right. Ignore the clamour of the touts at the beginning of the Corcovado road. They will try to convince you that the road is closed in order to take you on an alternative route and charge a hefty fee. If going by car to Corcovado, avoid going on weekends and public holidays – the slow traffic and long queues are overwhelming. Cars cannot go all the way to the parking outside the entrance, which is only for authorized cars and vans, instead you have to park halfway in a designated car park and then either walk or take a van (US$10 Monday-Friday, US$13 at weekends), although you have to pay for the van anyway. Avoid returning after dark; it is not safe. Parking space near the Trem do Corcovado is very limited.

Almost all the hotels, even the hostels, offer organized **coach trips** to Corcovado, which usually take in Sugar Loaf and Maracanã as well. These offer a fairly brief stop on the mountain and times of day are not always the best for light.

Helicopter tours are available, though these leave from the Sugar Loaf, the Dona Marta mirante or the Lagoa.

Cosme Velho

The **Museu Internacional de Arte Naïf do Brasil (MIAN)** ⓘ *R Cosme Velho 561, on the same street as the station for Corcovado, T021-2205 8612, Tue-Fri 1000-1800, US$6*, which re-opened in 2012 after renovation, is one of the most comprehensive museums of naïf and folk paintings in the world with a permanent collection of 8000 works by naïf artists from 130 countries. The museum also hosts several thematic and temporary exhibitions through the year. Parts of its collection are often on loan around the world. There is a coffee shop and a souvenir shop where you can buy paintings, books, postcards and T-shirts. Courses and workshops on painting and related subjects are also available.

The **Largo do Boticário** ⓘ *R Cosme Velho 822*, is a pretty, shady little square close to the terminus for the Corcovado cog railway and surrounded by 19th-century buildings. It offers a glimpse of what the city looked like before all the concrete and highways. That the square exists at all is thanks to concerned residents who not only sought to preserve it but were also instrumental in rebuilding and refurbishing many of the buildings, using rubble from colonial buildings demolished in the city centre. Many of the doors once belonged to churches. The four houses that front the square are painted different colours (white, pale blue, caramel and pink), each with features picked out in decorative tiles, woodwork and stone. Many artists live here and can often be seen painting in the courtyard.

Copacabana and Leme → *For listings, see pages 70-103.*

Copacabana, which is called Leme at its northern end, epitomizes picture-book Rio: a splendid broad sweeping crescent of fine sand stretching for almost 8 km, washed by a bottle-green Atlantic and watched over by the **Morro do Leme** – another of Rio's beautiful forest-covered hills. Behind it is a wide neon- and argon-lit avenue lined with high-rises, the odd grand hotel and various bars, restaurants and clubs. The tanned and toned flock all around in little bikinis, *sungas* and colourful beach wraps, playing volleyball on the sand and jogging along the wavy black and white dragon's tooth pavements, while others busk, play capoeira and sell their wares. Until the turn of the 21st century, Copacabana and Leme were a little tawdry. New beach cafés, paving, a clamp-down on the unpleasant street-walking and targeted policing have made the beach far and safer. While the water can be dirty when the currents wash shoreward, Copacabana and Leme are now as pleasant places to relax in the sun as neighbouring Ipanema. And they're a good deal cheaper.

Rio's sun worshippers

Ipanema and Copacabana are the most famous beaches in the world and there can surely be no people more devoted to lazing in the sun than Cariocas. But it wasn't always so. In the 19th century Brazilians would only go near sea water if they had been ordered to do so by a doctor. Even then it would only be for a quick dip at the beginning or the end of the day when the sun was weak. A tan was regarded as unhealthy and a sign of being lower class; to actually sit in the sun was a serious breach of social propriety.

All this began to change when the famous French actress Sarah Bernhardt came to Rio in 1886 to star in *Frou Frou* and *The Lady of the Camelias* at the São Pedro theatre. During her time off she caused a scandal, appalling the great and the good by travelling to then distant Copacabana, throwing on a swimsuit, sunbathing and even swimming in the sea. By the turn of the 20th century others had begun to follow suit, and by 1917 going to the beach had become sufficiently fashionable that the city established strict rules and regulations to govern sun worship. People were permitted to bathe only between 0500-0800 and 1700-1900, had to wear appropriate dress and be quiet and discreet; failure to do so resulted in five years in prison. Official attitudes only began to change in the 1920s with the building of the Copacabana Palace and the arrival of more foreigners who ignored Rio's prudishness and convinced Cariocas to begin to enjoy the beach.

Arriving in Copacabana and Leme

Buses are plentiful and cost US$2.70; Nos 119, 154, 413, 415, 455 and 474 run between the city centre and Avenida Nossa Senhora de Copacabana. If you are going to the centre from Copacabana, look for 'Castelo', 'Praça XV', 'E Ferro' or 'Praça Mauá' on the sign by the front door. 'Aterro' means the expressway between Botafogo and downtown Rio (not open on Sunday). From the centre to Copacabana is easier as all buses in that direction are clearly marked. The 'Aterro' bus takes 15 minutes. Numerous buses and minivans run between Copacabana and Ipanema; the two beaches are connected by Rua Francisco Otaviano or Rua Joaquim Nabuco, immediately west of the Forte de Copacabana. Copacabana has *metrô* stations a few blocks inland from the beach at Cardeal Arcoverde, Siqueira Campos and Cantagalo. Copacabana *metrô* is linked to Lapa, the centre and Ipanema.

Places in Copacabana and Leme

Copacabana has always been a beach and beyond it there are few sights of any note. The area exploded in population after the construction of the **Túnel**

Velho (Old Tunnel) in 1891 and the **New Tunnel** in the early 20th century and has been growing, mostly upward, ever since. Streets are lined with high-rise flats that huddle together even on the seafront, crowding around the stately neoclassical façade of the **Copacabana Palace** hotel, which was the tallest building in the suburb until the 1940s.

Apart from New Year's Eve, when the whole suburb becomes a huge party venue and bands play along the entire length of the beach, Copacabana is a place for little more than landscape and people-watching. It's possible to swim in the sea when the current is heading out from the shore. At other times check on water quality with the lifeguards and the various lifeguard stations (*postos*) that line the beach. The best way to enjoy the area is to wander along the

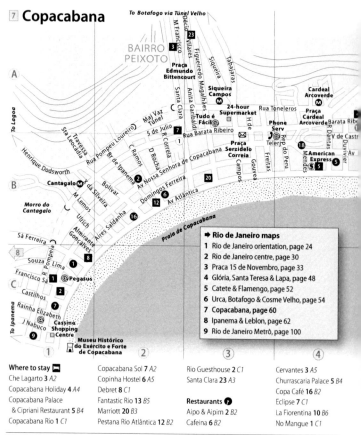

Copacabana

➡ **Rio de Janeiro maps**
1 Rio de Janeiro orientation, page 24
2 Rio de Janeiro centre, page 30
3 Praca 15 de Novembro, page 33
4 Glória, Santa Teresa & Lapa, page 48
5 Catete & Flamengo, page 52
6 Urca, Botafogo & Cosme Velho, page 54
7 Copacabana, page 60
8 Ipanema & Leblon, page 62
9 Rio de Janeiro Metrô, page 100

Where to stay 🛏
Che Lagarto **3** *A2*
Copacabana Holiday **4** *A4*
Copacabana Palace
 & Cipriani Restaurant **5** *B4*
Copacabana Rio **1** *C1*

Copacabana Sol **7** *A2*
Copinha Hostel **6** *A5*
Debret **8** *C1*
Fantastic Rio **13** *B5*
Marriott **20** *B3*
Pestana Rio Atlântica **12** *B2*

Rio Guesthouse **2** *C1*
Santa Clara **23** *A3*

Restaurants 🍴
Aipo & Aipim **2** *B2*
Cafeina **6** *B2*

Cervantes **3** *A5*
Churrascaria Palace **5** *B4*
Copa Café **16** *B2*
Eclipse **7** *C1*
La Fiorentina **10** *B6*
No Mangue **1** *C1*

dragon-tooth paved promenade, perhaps stopping to enjoy a coconut at one of the numerous beachfront snack bars, and noting the different crowd at each one. Everyone looks at everyone else in Rio so don't be afraid to do the same.

At the far end of the beach is the **Museu Histórico do Exército e Forte de Copacabana** ① *Av Atlântica at Francisco Otaviano, Posto 6, T021-2521 1032, www.fortedecopacabana.com, Tue-Sun and bank holidays 1000-1800, US$5*, a museum charting the history of the army in Brazil through the colonial, imperial and republican periods, with cases of military artefacts and panels in Portuguese on campaigns such as the one fought at Canudos against Antônio Conselheiro. There are good views out over the beaches from the fort and a small restaurant. A new, state-of-the-art **Museu da Imagem e do Som do Rio** ① *www.mis.rj.gov.br (see page 34)* is due to open in Copacabana in time for the 2014 FIFA World Cup™.

Ipanema and Leblon

→ *For listings, see pages 70-103.*

Like Copacabana and Leme, Ipanema and Leblon are essentially one long curving beach enclosed by the monolithic Dois Irmãos rocks at the western end and the Arpoador rocks to the east. And, like Copacabana and Leme, they have few sights beyond the sand, the landscape and the beautiful people. Ipanema and Leblon have long regarded themselves as Rio's most fashionable and cool stretches of sand. If Copacabana is samba, then Ipanema and Leblon are bossa nova: wealthy, pricey, predominantly white, and sealed off from the realities of Rio in a neat little fairy-tale strip of streets, watched over by twinkling lights high up on the flanks of the Morro Dois Irmãos. They look so romantic that it is easy to forget that they come from one of the city's largest *favelas*.

Siri Mole & Cia **9** *C1*
Traiteurs de France **18** *B4*

Shop ☺
Modern Sound **1** *B2*

Bars & clubs ♥
Clandestino **19** *A4*

Costly, closeted and cosseted though they may be, these are the beach suburbs in which to base yourself whilst in Rio if you're in the money. Almost all of the city's best restaurants and high-end shops are here (and in the suburbs of Gávea and Lagoa, which lie behind). The streets are fairly clean and usually walked by nothing more dangerous than a small white poodle, the sea is good for swimming and the only beach hotels of any character lie in here.

Arriving in Ipanema and Leblon

General Osório *metrô* station in Ipanema was closed for renovation in 2013, but is due to open for the 2014 FIFA World Cup™. Express 'Metro do Superficie' buses run from Ipanema/General Osório to Gávea along the beachfront

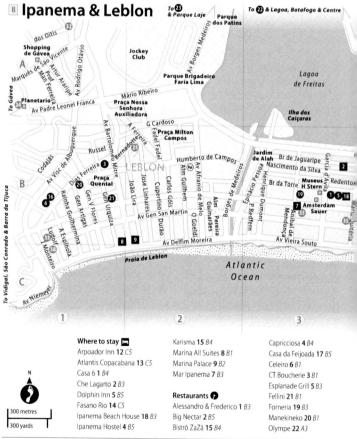

8 Ipanema & Leblon

Where to stay 🛏
Arpoador Inn **12** C5
Atlantis Copacabana **13** C5
Casa 6 **1** B4
Che Lagarto **2** B3
Dolphin Inn **5** B5
Fasano Rio **14** C5
Ipanema Beach House **18** B3
Ipanema Hostel **4** B5

Karisma **15** B4
Marina All Suites **8** B1
Marina Palace **9** B2
Mar Ipanema **7** B3

Restaurants 🍴
Alessandro & Frederico **1** B3
Big Nectar **2** B5
Bistrô ZaZá **15** B4

Capricciosa **4** B4
Casa da Feijoada **17** B5
Celeiro **6** B1
CT Boucherie **3** B1
Esplanade Grill **5** B3
Fellini **21** B1
Forneria **19** B3
Manekineko **20** B1
Olympe **22** A3

N
300 metres
300 yards

Rua Visconde de Pirajá in Ipanema and Avenida Ataulfo de Paiva in Leblon. Minivans run between the centre and/or Leme and Leblon, along the seafront roads. Bus destinations are clearly marked but, as a rule of thumb, any buses heading east along the seafront go to Copacabana or, if going west, to Barra da Tijuca; those going inland will pass by the Lagoa or Gávea. See map, page 24, and www.rioonibus.com for more details.

Places in Ipanema and Leblon

Like Copacabana, Ipanema and Leblon are places for people-watching. A few hours wandering around Ipanema/Leblon followed by a half-day wandering Copacabana/Leme can be most interesting. The crowds are quite different.

Polis Sucos 7 *B3*
Porcão 13 *B4*
Roberta Sudbrack 23 *A2*
Satyricon 8 *B4*
Zuka 16 *B1*

Bars & clubs 🎵
00 (Zero Zero) 24 *A1*
Academia da Cachaça 25 *B2*

Bar Lagoa 37 *B4*
Barril 1800 27 *C5*
Devassa 33 *B1 & B3*
Empório 35 *B3*
Garota de Ipanema 36 *B4*
Hipódromo de Gávea 32 *A1*
Melt 38 *C1*
Shenanigans 40 *B5*
Vinícius 42 *B4*

Shop 🎵
Toca do Vinicius 1 *B4*

➡ **Rio de Janeiro maps**
1 Rio de Janeiro orientation, page 24
2 Rio de Janeiro centre, page 30
3 Praca 15 de Novembro, page 33
4 Glória, Santa Teresa & Lapa, page 48
5 Catete & Flamengo, page 52
6 Urca, Botafogo & Cosme Velho, page 54
7 Copacabana, page 60
8 Ipanema & Leblon, page 62

While Copacabana attracts a real cross-section of Rio society, Ipanema and Leblon are predominantly haunts of the fashionable peacocks, who strut along the beachfront promenade, especially around **Posto Nove**. Beyond the people and the breathtaking landscape, there is little to see here but plenty to do, especially for avid consumers. Shopping is best on and around Rua Visconde de Piraja and Rua Garcia D'Avila, where you'll find famous Rio brands like Lenny, Salinas, Blue Man and Oh Boy (see Shopping, page 90), and at the **Feira Hippy** (see Markets, page 91), where you will find everything from high-quality Brazilian designer swimwear to seed bracelets and T-shirts with pictures of Bob Marley. Those seeking culture but unwilling to leave the beach should head for the **Casa de Cultura Laura Alvim** ① *Av Vieira Souto 176, T021-7104 3603, www.casadelaura.com.br*, comprising an arts cinema, art galleries (temporary exhibitions), workshop spaces and a bookshop. If it is pouring with rain you could watch diamonds being cut and set at the **Museus H Stern** ① *R Garcia D'Avila 113, T021-2106 0000*, or **Amsterdam Sauer** ① *R Garcia D'Avila 105, T021-2512 1132*, or hang out in the **Garota de Ipanema**, the bar where the *Girl from Ipanema* was written in the late 1950s (see Bars and clubs, page 83).

Gávea, Lagoa and Jardim Botânico → *For listings, see pages 70-103.*

Just inland from Ipanema and Leblon, nestled under the forested slopes of Corcovado and the Tijuca National Park and spread around the picturesque saltwater lagoon of Lagoa Rodrigo de Freitas, are these three mainly residential suburbs. There are a few sights of interest and all have lively top-end nightlife. **Gávea** tends to attract the young and wealthy, while the 30-somethings dine in the restaurants in **Lagoa** overlooking the lagoon and go out to clubs in **Leblon** or to the exclusive **Jockey Club**.

Arriving in Gávea, Lagoa and Jardim Botânico
Buses from the centre are marked 'Gávea', or for the Jardim Botânico, Leblon, Gávea or São Conrado 'via Jóquei'. Bus Nos 571 and 170 from the centre go to the Jardim Botânico or No 172 from Flamengo or Botafogo. Bus No 584 runs between Jardim Botânico and Copacabana. Bus Nos 176 and 178 run from the centre and Flamengo and bus Nos 591 and 592 from Copacabana go to the planetarium.

Lagoa de Freitas
The lagoa is another of Rio de Janeiro's unfeasibly beautiful natural sights and has long been admired. Darwin and German naturalists Spix and Martius mention it in their accounts. It is best seen in the early evening when thick

golden sunlight bathes the rainforest-clad slopes of the **Serra da Carioca**, which rise high above it to reach their spectacular pinnacle with the distant xenon-white statue of Christ.

Like Copacabana and Guanabara Bay, it could be even more beautiful if only it were looked after a little better. The canal that links the lake to the sea is far too narrow to allow for sufficient exchange of water; pollution makes it unsafe for swimming and occasional summer algal blooms have led to mass fish deaths.

The lake is surrounded by a series of parks. Immediately next to it is the **Parque Tom Jobim** and contiguous are **Brigadeiro Faria Lima**, **Parque do Cantagalo** and **Parque das Taboas**. All have extensive leisure areas popular with roller skaters and volleyball players. There are live shows and *forró* dancing in the **Parque dos Patins** and kiosks serve a variety of food from Arabic to Japanese. Nearby is the **Parque Carlos Lacerda** ① *Av Epitacio Pessoa, daily 0800-1900*, an open-air art gallery with sculptures by local artists in a landscaped park shaded by ornamental trees.

Jardim Botânico (botanical gardens)
① *R Jardim Botânico 1008, T021-3874 1808, www.jbrj.gov.br, daily 0800-1700, US$3.50.*

These extensive 137-ha gardens protect 9000 rare vascular plants and are home to 140 species of birds, and butterflies including the brilliant blue morphos. There are stately stands of 40-m-high royal palms, large tropical ficus and ceiba trees and pau brasil, from which the country gets its name. Giant Amazonian Victoria regia lilies cover many of the ponds and there are views up to Corcovado through the trees. The gardens were founded in 1808 by the king, Dom Joao VI, as a nursery for European plants and new specimens from throughout the world. When the electric tram line arrived in this part of the city, housing and industries soon followed, but the gardens, then as now, remained a haven of peace. There is a herbarium, an aquarium and a library as well as the **Museu Botânico**, housing exhibitions on the conservation of Brazilian flora, and the **Casa dos Pilões**, the first gun-powder factory in Brazil. A new pavilion contains sculptures by Mestre Valentim. Many improvements were carried out before the 1992 Earth Summit, including a new *orquidario*, an enlarged bookshop and a smart café. Birdwatchers can expect to see rarities including the social flycatcher, great and boat-billed kiskadees, cattle tyrants, sayaca, palm and seven-coloured (green-headed) tanagers as well as over 20 different kinds of hummingbird, roadside hawks, laughing falcons and various toucans and parakeets. There are marmosets in the trees.

Less than 1 km from the gardens is the little-visited **Parque Laje** ① *R Jardim Botânico 414, daily 0900-1700, free*, which is more jungle-like than the Jardim Botânico and has a series of small grottoes, an old tower and lakes, as well as the **Escola de Artes Visuais** (visual arts school) housed in a large colonial house in the grounds.

The **Planetário** ⓘ *R Padre Leonel Franco 240, Gávea, www.rio.rj.gov.br/planetario, by appointment, free*, has a sculpture of the Earth and Moon by Mário Agostinelli. On Wednesday evenings at dusk, in clear weather, astronomers give guided observations of the stars. At weekends there are shows for children at 1630, 1800 and 1930. There are occasional *chorinho* concerts on Thursday or Friday.

Rough paths lead to the summit of the flat-topped **Pedra da Gávea** and to magnificent views. Hang-gliders fly to the beach at São Conrado from the **Pedra Bonita** behind the Pedra da Gávea. ▸▸ *See What to do, page 93.*

Barra da Tijuca and beyond → *For listings, see pages 70-103.*

This rapidly developing district, modelled on Miami, is one of the city's principal middle class residential areas. It focuses on a 20-km sandy beach that is renowned for its surfing, especially at its far westernmost end: **Recreio dos Bandeirantes**. There are countless bars and restaurants, concentrated at both ends, as well as campsites, motels and hotels, built in increasing number in anticipation of the 2016 Olympics. Budget accommodation tends to be self-catering. The neighbourhoods were planned and built for the car. Walking distances are long and the neighbourhood feels characterless and lacking in intimacy compared to the rest of Rio.

Arriving in Barra da Tijuca
Buses from the city centre to Barra are Nos 175 and 176; from Botafogo, Glória or Flamengo take No 179; from Leme Nos 591 or 592; and from Copacabana via Leblon No 523 (45 minutes to one hour). A taxi from the centre costs US$25 (US$32 after 2400) or US$15 from Ipanema. A comfortable bus, **Pegasus**, goes along the coast from the Castelo bus terminal to Barra da Tijuca and continues to Campo Grande or Santa Cruz; or take the free 'Barra Shopping' bus. Bus No 700 from Praça São Conrado runs the full length of the beach to Recreio dos Bandeirantes.

Places in Barra da Tijuca
The **Bosque da Barra/Parque Arruda Câmara** ⓘ *junction of Av das Américas and Av Ayrton Senna, daily 0700-1700*, preserves the vegetation of the sandbanks that existed on this part of the coast before the city took over. The **Autódromo** (motor-racing track) is behind Barra and the Lagoa de Jacarepaguá, in the district of the same name. The Brazilian Grand Prix was held here during the 1980s before returning to Interlagos, São Paulo.

A bit further out is the **Museu Casa do Pontal** ⓘ *Estrada do Pontal 3295, Recreio dos Bandeirantes, T021-2490 3278, www.museucasadopontal.com.br,*

A model favela

In the late 1990s, in an attempt to escape *favela* Pereira da Silva's mixture of boredom and sporadic violence, Cilan Souza de Oliveira, his brother and their schoolboy friends created a model of their home on a patch of wasteland at the edge of the community. "Soon all the kids began to get involved and we gave the play area a name – Morrinho." Painted breeze blocks served as model houses, dolls and toy cars gave the model life and soon Morrinho had spread to cover an entire small hillside. "Then the media started to come and the *favela* started to get famous for Morrinho instead of violence," recalls Cilan, "Even the police changed their attitude. As we turned from children to teenagers they started to treat us differently –

'so you're the kids who built Morrinho?' they'd ask, impressed rather than suspicious. Then people started to call us artists. And we realized we'd made a model of our reality – our world in miniature – from the baile funk parties to the gangs and police raids." Morrinho is now a tourist attraction and the seat of an international NGO (www.morrinho.com) and *favela* Pereira da Silva has become one of Rio's least troubled. "It's great when tourists come," says Cilan. "They arrive full of fear and apprehension, and leave thinking that we have a wonderful community. Three foreigners who came as visitors have now moved in to the *favela* and one had become a baile funk rapper. We call him MC Gringo!"

Tue-Sun 0930-1700. Located in a little wood near Recreio dos Bandeirantes beach, this is one of the finest collections of Brazilian folk art in the country. There are over 5000 works by more than 200 artists from 24 different Brazilian states, accumulated French designer Jacques van de Beuque over a 40-year period. Recommended.

Parque Nacional da Tijuca → *For listings, see pages 70-103. See map, page 24.*

ⓘ *Daily 0600-2100.*

Corcovado is situated within Tijuca National Park; one of the largest areas of urban rainforest in the world. It is a haven for city-weary Cariocas, as well as for some 200 species of birds, numerous small mammals and primates and hundreds of species of endangered Atlantic coast rainforest plants. The forest has a number of natural springs, many of which have been diverted through bamboo channels to form natural showers – be sure to bring swimming gear. There is plenty of shade and the views from the various vantage points are almost as impressive as those from Corcovado.

The vegetation in the Parque Nacional da Tijuca is not primary; most is natural regrowth and planned reforestation. It is a testament to what humans can do to regenerate lost forest. The first Europeans to arrive in the area cut down trees for use in construction and as firewood. The lower areas were cleared to make way for sugar plantations. When coffee was introduced to Rio de Janeiro in 1760 further swathes were cut down for *fazendas*. But the deforestation destroyed Rio's watershed and in 1861, in one of the world's first conservation projects, the imperial government decided that Tijuca should become a rainforest preserve. The enormous task of reforesting the entire area was given to an army major, Manuel Gomes Archer, who took saplings from other areas of Atlantic forest and replanted Tijuca with native trees and a selection of exotics in fewer than 13 years. The names of the six slaves who did the actual manual work is not known. Reforestation was continued by Tomas de Gama. In 1961 Tijuca was joined to several other patches of remnant forest to form a national park of 3300 ha.

Arriving in Parque Nacional da Tijuca

To get to the park entrance, take bus No 221 from Praça 15 de Novembro, No 233 ('Barra da Tijuca') or No 234 from the *rodoviária* or No 454 from Copacabana to Alto da Boa Vista. There is no public transport within the park and the best way to explore is by trail, tour, bicycle or car. If hiking in the park other than on the main paths, a guide may be useful if you do not want to get lost. Contact the **Sindicato de Guías** ① *T021-267 4582.* ›› *See Hiking, page 94.*

Places in Parque Nacional da Tijuca

One of the best walks is to the **Pico da Tijuca** (1022 m). Views from the top are wonderful and the walk offers the chance to see plenty of animals. Allow two to three hours. To get to the trailhead enter the park at **Alto da Boa Vista** and follow the signposts (maps are displayed) to **Bom Retiro**, a good picnic place (1½ hours' walk). At Bom Retiro the road ends and it is another hour's walk up a fair footpath to the summit (take the path from the right of the Bom Retiro drinking fountain, not the more obvious steps from the left). The last part consists of steps carved out of the solid rock. There are several sheer drops at the summit which are masked by bushes – be wary. The route is shady for almost its entire length. The main path to Bom Retiro passes the **Cascatinha Taunay** (a 30-m waterfall) and the **Mayrink Chapel** (1860). Panels painted in the Chapel by Cândido Portinari have been replaced by copies and the originals will probably be installed in the Museu de Arte Moderna. Beyond the chapel is the wonderful little restaurant Os Esquilos, which dates from 1945. Allow at least five hours for the walk.

Other viewpoints include the **Paulo e Virginia Grotto**, the **Vista do Almirante**, the **Mesa do Imperador** and the **Vista Chinesa** (420 m), a Chinese-style pavilion with a view of the Lagoa Rodrigo de Freitas, Ipanema and Leblon.

Museu Açude ① *Estrada do Açude 764, Alto da Boa Vista, T021-2492 2119, www. museuscastromaya.com.br, Thu-Sun 1100-1700, Sun brunch with live music 1230-1700*, is in the former home of tycoon Castro Maia with some impressive murals and *azulejos* (tiles).

Western Rio: beyond Barra → *For listings, see pages 70-103.*

Almost half of the municipal area of Rio de Janeiro is in what is referred to as the **Zona Oeste** (West Zone), a region that stretches along the coast beyond Barra da Tijuca in a succession of surf beaches. These include **Prainha** and **Grumari**, both of which are broad sweeps of sand backed by rugged hills and dotted with rustic beach bars. Neither are accessible by public transport and both are busy at weekends. Further west still are the **Barra de Guaratiba** and **Pedra de Guaratiba** beaches and, finally, those at **Sepetiba**. This stunning coastal road (the start of the Costa Verde highway) is becoming obliterated by executive housing developments, so visit soon.

Sítio Roberto Burle Marx ① *Estrada da Barra de Guaratiba 2019, Barra de Guaratiba, T021-2410 1171, daily 0930-1330, by appointment only*, was, from 1949 to 1994, the home of the great Roberto Burle Marx (1909-1994), world famous as a landscape designer and artist. His projects achieved a rare harmony between nature, architecture and man-made landscapes. He created many schemes in Brazil and abroad; in Rio alone his work includes the Parque do Flamengo, the pavements of the Avenida Atlântica in Copacabana, Praça Júlio de Noronha in Leme, the remodelling of the Largo da Carioca, the gardens of the Museu Nacional de Belas-Artes and of the Biblioteca Nacional and the complex at the Santa Teresa tram station near the Catedral Metropolitana.

Covering 350,000 sq m, the estate contains an estimated 3500 species of plants, mostly Brazilian. It is run now by the **Instituto do Patrimônio Histórico e Artístico Nacional (IPHAN)** and one of its main aims is to produce seedlings of the plants in its collection. Also on view are Burle Marx's collection of paintings, ceramics, sculptures and other objets d'art, plus examples of his own designs and paintings. The library houses 2500 volumes on botany, architecture and landscape design.

The 12,500-ha **Parque Estadual da Pedra Branca** ① *www.inea.rj.gov.br/ unidades/pqpedra_branca.asp, Tue-Sun 0800-1700, free*, which lies inland of western Rio, is the largest stretch of urban forest in Rio (a claim often erroneously made for Parque Nacional da Tijuca) and the second largest in the world after the Serra da Cantareira in Sao Paulo (which, unlike Pedra Branca, is not flanked entirely by urban areas). The park focuses on the 1025-m-high Pedra Branca and preserves numerous important Mata Atlântica species. Visits can be arranged through the **Amigos do Parque** ① *www.parquepedrabranca.com.*

Rio de Janeiro city listings

For hotel and restaurant price codes and other relevant information, see pages 9-13.

🔲 Where to stay

The best places to stay in Rio are **Copacabana**, **Leblon**, **Ipanema**, the **Arpoador** and **Santa Teresa**. The first 4 (which are contiguous) are great for the beach; Santa Teresa is best for nightlife, culture and easy access to Lapa, the Sambódromo and Carnaval. Ipanema is probably the safest area in the city. Those looking for hotels with charm and personality will find Rio unremarkable. With a few notable exceptions, those in the higher and mid-range bracket are a mix of anonymous business chain towers and fading leftovers from the 1970s, complete with period decor. Those at the lower end are all too often dubious hot-pillow establishments in equally dubious areas. Guesthouses and B&Bs are a far better option even for those on a medium budget. Backpackers are well catered for. Searches on sites such as www.hostels.com or www.hostelworld.com will yield almost 50 options and numbers are increasing every month. There are far too many for us to list them all here, so we have only included our favourites.

Accommodation prices increase significantly over New Year and Carnaval, when they are among the most expensive in the world, soaring above equivalents in New York or London. Reserve well in advance.

Self-catering apartments

Self-catering apartments are a popular and good-value form of accommodation in Rio, available at all price levels. In Flamengo furnished apartments for short-term let, accommodating up to 6, cost from US$300 per month. In Copacabana, Ipanema and Leblon prices start at about US$25 a day (US$500-600 a month) for a simple studio, up to US$2500 a month for a luxurious residence sleeping 4-6. Heading south past Barra da Tijuca, virtually all the accommodation available is self-catering. Renting a small flat, or sharing a larger one, can be much better value than a hotel room.

Blocks consisting entirely of short-let apartments can attract thieves, so check the (usually excellent) security arrangements. Residential buildings are called '*prédio familial*'. Higher floors ('*alto andar*') are quieter.

See websites such as www.aluguetemporada.com.br, www.riotemporada.net and www.vivareal.com.br for more details. 'Apart-Hotels' are also listed in the *Guia 4 Rodas* and **Riotur**'s booklet. Agents and private owners advertise under '*Apartamentos – Temporada*' in publications like *Balcão* (twice weekly), *O Globo* or *Jornal do Brasil* (daily); advertisements are classified by district and size of apartment: '*vagas e quartos*' means shared accommodation; '*conjugado*' (or '*conj*') is a studio with limited cooking facilities; '*3 quartos*' is a 3-bedroom flat. There should always be a written agreement when renting.

Homestays and guesthouses

Many visitors choose to stay in family guesthouses or through homestay schemes. The former are listed in the text below; the latter are available through international schemes like www.airbnb.com (paid) or www.couchsurfing.org (free), though value-for-money/quality can be hard to come by. More reliable are locally run operators. These include:

$$$$-$$$ Hidden Pousadas Brazil, www.hiddenpousadasbrazil.com. Great accommodation options in carefully selected small mid- to upper-end hotels and homes throughout Rio and beyond. These include lovely properties in Leblon, Ipanema, Copacabana and Santa Teresa.

$$$$-$$ Bed and Breakfast, www.bedandbreakfast.com. With locations in Rio and throughout the world.

$$$$-$$ Cama e Café and **Rio Homestay**, R Laurinda Santos Lobo 124, Santa Teresa, T021-2225 4366, T021-9638 4850 (mob, 24 hrs), www.camaecafe.com and www.riohomestay.com. One of the best accommodation options in Rio with a range of more than 50 homestay deals in Santa Teresa, Cosme Velho and Ipanema from the simple to the luxurious.

Santa Teresa *p47, map p48*

$$$$ Mama Ruisa, R Santa Cristina 132, T021-2242 1281, www.mamaruisa.com. French-run boutique hotel with carefully casual public spaces and 4 simply decorated, elegant hard wood and whitewash rooms decorated in a modern French colonial style and named in homage to French artistic icons.

$$$ Casa Cool Beans, R Laurinda Santos Lobo 136, T021-2262 0552, with another branch in Ipanema, www.casacoolbeans.com. Situated in a large Santa Teresa town house on a quiet backstreet, decorated with art and graffiti by local artists, with a small pool, spacious wood-floored rooms and a generous breakfast.

$$$ Quinta Azul, R Almirante Alexandrino 256, T021-3253 1021, www.quintaazul.com. Cosy little boutique hotel with sweeping views from the upper rooms. Well situated. Small pool.

$$ Casa Áurea, R Áurea 80, T021-2242 5830, www.casaaurea.com.br. Tranquil, friendly, arty hostel and boutique hotel in a colonial house in a Santa Teresa backstreet. All rooms vary in shape, size and colour and they and the public spaces, which include a large garden patio, are decorated with tasteful art and craftwork.

$$ Rio Forest Hostel, R Joaquim Murtinho 517, T021-3563 1021, www.rioforesthostel.com.br. Bright, airy hostel with dorms and rooms with a view. Decent showers, friendly and welcoming staff and Wi-Fi throughout. Be sure to get to breakfast early if the hostel is fully booked to ensure a table.

$$ Rio Hostel, R Joaquim Murtinho 361, T021-3852 0827, www.riohostel.com. One of Rio's best small hostels. Clinging to the side of a hill, it has spectacular views of the centre and is on the doorstep of the city's best nightlife.

Glória, Catete and Flamengo

p50, maps p48 and p52

Primarily residential areas between the centre and Copacabana, with good bus and *metrô* connections. Glória, Catete and Flamengo lie next to a park landscaped by Burle Marx and a beautiful beach lapped by a filthy sea.

$$$$ Novo Mundo, Praia Flamengo 20, Catete, T021-2105 7000, www. hotelnovomundo.com.br. The 4-star price belies this (newly renovated) art deco dame's 3-star fittings (plastic shower curtains, tiny gym), but the views of the Sugar Loaf from the bay-facing rooms and the proximity to the centre and Santos Dumont Airport make this a good business choice.

$$$$ Windsor Flórida, R Ferreira Viana 81, Catete, T021-2195 6800, www.windsorhoteis.com. Corporate-oriented hotel with a well-equipped business centre, one of the city's largest convention centres, bars (for private hire), a restaurant and modestly decorated no-nonsense modern rooms with Wi-Fi.

$$ Imperial, R do Catete 186, Catete, T021-2112 6000, www.imperialhotel. com.br. One of the city's very first grand hotels, built in the late 19th century. Rooms are divided between the old building and the new annex. The latter has modern US-style motel rooms.

Botafogo and Urca *p53, map p54*

$$ Alpha Hostel, R Praia de Botafogo 462, casa 3, T021-2286 7799, www. alphahostel.com. Small-scale hostel in a pretty little townhouse with pocket-sized but well-kept a/c rooms.

$$ El Misti Hostel, Praia de Botafogo 462, casa 9, Botafogo, T021-2226 0991, www.elmistihostel.com. A converted colonial house with 6 dorms, shared bathrooms, kitchen and internet, capoeira classes and tour service. Popular with party-goers.

$$ Sun Rio Hostel, R Praia de Botafogo 462, casa 5, Botafogo, next door to **El Misti**, T021-2226 0461, www.sunriohostel.com.br. A/c dorms, doubles and en suites, all very well kept and clean. Shared kitchen, internet, bike rental and tours organized. Friendly owner Daniela is very welcoming.

Copacabana and Leme *p58, maps p60 and p62*

Many hotels charge about 30% more for a sea view, but some town-side upper rooms have good views of the mountains.

$$$$ Copacabana Palace, Av Atlântica 1702, T021-2548 7070, www.copacabanapalace.com.br. Made famous by Ginger Rogers and Fred Astaire, who filmed *Flying down to Rio* here. Rooms are quiet, spacious and comfortable, with superb beds, effortless service, and conservative and rather European decor. The hotel restaurant, **Cipriani**, is of a similar high standard to its celebrated sister restaurants in Venice and New York.

$$$$ Copacabana Rio, Av N S de Copacabana 1256, T021-2267 9900, www.copacabanariohotel.com.br. Quiet, efficiently run 1970s tower with simple but well-maintained standard 3-star rooms.

$$$$ Marriott, Av Atlântica 2600, T021-2545 6500, www.marriott.com. 245 guest rooms specifically designed for the business traveller, an executive floor, 12 meeting rooms and a whole gamut of other business services.

$$$$ Pestana Rio Atlântica, Av Atlântica 2964, T021-2548 6332, www.pestana.com. Spacious bright rooms and a rooftop pool and terrace with sweeping views. Very high standards. Highly recommended.

$$$ Atlantis Copacabana, Av Bulhões de Carvalho 61, T021-2521 1142, www.atlantishotel.com.br. Newly renovated Arpoador hotel in a quiet, safe street very close to the beach. Small rooftop pool, sauna and Wi-Fi.

$$$ Copacabana Sol, R Santa Clara 141, T021-2549 4577, www.copacabanasolhotel.com.br. Tiled, a/c rooms with cable TV, Wi-Fi, safes and en suite bathrooms with marble commodes and showers. Good value.

$$$ Debret, Av Atlântica 3564, T021-2522 0132, www.debret.com. Bright, spacious, modern seafront rooms in pastel colours; others are a little dark. Free Wi-Fi. Separate restaurant.

$$$ Rio Guesthouse, R Francisco Sa 5, T021-2521 8568, www.rioguesthouse.com. Modest but comfortable a/c rooms in the top floor apartment of a tall building overlooking the beach. Superb views. Friendly and helpful.

$$$ Santa Clara, R Décio Vilares 316, Metrô Siqueira Campos, T021-2256 2650, www.hotelsantaclara.com.br. Bright, newly refurbished rooms a few blocks back from the beach. Well maintained, discreet and good value, at the lower end of this price range.

$$ Che Lagarto Copacabana, R Barata Ribeiro 111, T021-3209 0348, www.chelagarto.com. Very popular and well-run hostel with spacious, clean dorms and doubles, a lovely pool and bar on the terrace and one of the best ranges of tours in Rio, including surf classes. Excellent English spoken. Taken over by the Argentine chain in 2012.

$$ Copinha Hostel, R Felipe de Oliveira 11, T021-2275 8520, www.copinhahostel.com.br. Clean, well-run little lemon-yellow hostel with a range of a/c dorms and doubles in white tile and with en suites. 24-hr reception, kitchen, cable TV and transport services.

Self-catering apartments

Copacabana Holiday, R Barata Ribeiro 90A, T021-2542 1525, www.copacabanaholiday.com.br. Recommended, well-equipped small apartments from US$500 per month, minimum 30-day let.

Fantastic Rio, Av Atlântica 974, apt 501, Leme, T021-3507 7491, http://fantasticrio.br.tripod.com. All types of furnished accommodation from US$20 per day. Good service, contact Peter Corr.

Ipanema and Leblon *p61, map p62*

$$$$ Fasano Rio, Av Vieira Souto 80, Ipanema, T021-3202 4000, www.fasano.com.br. This Philippe Starck-designed luxury hotel in the tasteful Paulistano hotel chain is by far the best in Ipanema and, aside from **La Suite** in Barra da Tijuca, the best in Rio. The superior **Fasano Al Mare** restaurant serves delicious Italian seafood. There's a spectacular rooftop terrace, pool, fitness centre, sauna and massage, a good bar with live music, and limousine service for airport transfers.

$$$$ Marina Palace and **Marina All Suites**, Av Delfim Moreira 630 and 696, Ipanema, T021-2294 1794, www.hotelmarina.com.br. 2 towers of 1980s vintage almost next door to each other. The former has smart, modern but standard 4-star rooms, a rooftop pool and occasional discount rates over the internet, the latter is a luxury boutique with designer suites and is favoured by the likes of Giselle Bündchen. By international standards it is shabby, but it has an excellent and fashionable sea-view restaurant and bar which is great for breakfast and a light lunch or dinner.

$$$ Arpoador Inn, Francisco Otaviano 177, Ipanema, T021-2523 0060, www.arpoadorinn.com.br. One of the best deals on the seafront. Well maintained, with off-season special offers. Recommended.

$$$ Dolphin Inn, R Bulhões de Carvalho 480, Casa 6 Ipanema, T021-9672 0025, www.bedandbreakfast. com/brazil-rio-de-janeiro-riodolphin inn-page.html. This delightful private house in a safe, quiet, gated street less than 5 mins from the *metrô* and Ipanema and Copacabana beaches, can be rented in whole or part. The American and Carioca surfer owners are warm, welcoming and their home reflects their exuberant personalities. Book well ahead.

$$$ Ipanema Inn, Maria Quitéria 27, behind Caesar Park, Ipanema, T021-2523 6092, www.ipanemainn.com.br.

A popular package tour and small business hotel less than 100 m from the beach. Good value and location.

$$$ Mar Ipanema, R Visconde de Pirajá 539, Ipanema, T021-3875 9190, www.maripanema.com. Simple, smart, modern rooms a block from the beach. The front rooms can be noisy.

$$ Casa 6, R Barão da Torre 175, casa 6, Ipanema, T021-2247 1384, www.casa6ipanema.com. This French-owned B&B in 2 townhouses sits on a street filled with hostels, 3 blocks from the beach. It offers good long-stay rates and the small rooms with en suites are decorated in wood and tile and fan-cooled.

$$ Che Lagarto, R Barão de Jaguaripe 208, Ipanema, T021-2247 4582, www.chelagarto.com. Bright red, bustling party hostel with young staff and a terrace with views of Corcovado. Dorms and doubles.

$$ Ipanema Beach House, R Barão da Torre 485, Ipanema, T021-3203 3693, www.ipanemahouse.com. Great little hostel with very friendly staff, pool, internet, outdoor bar, Continental breakfast, a range of dorms and doubles, 24-hr check-in.

$$ Ipanema Hostel, R Canning, casa 1, Ipanema, T021-2287 2928, www. riohostelipanema.com. Sister hostel to the friendly and welcoming **Rio Hostel** in Santa Teresa with a range of small rooms and dorms, a tour operator, internet and a lively crowd.

$$ Karisma, R Barão da Torre 177, Ipanema, T021-2523 1372, www. karismahostel.com. Tranquil little hostel 3 blocks from the beach, small but well-kept dorms and pokey doubles, all up a steep flight of stairs. English spoken, lockers, internet and kitchen.

Gávea p64
$$$$ La Maison, R Sergio Porto 58, T021-3205 3585, www.lamaisonario. com. Rio's only other decent boutique hotel, also run by the French owners of **La Suite**, sits in a period town house on a quiet backstreet in this residential suburb. The bright spacious rooms are tastefully decorated in primary colours and there are wonderful views of Corcovado from the open-sided breakfast area and the little pool. The beach is a taxi ride away.

Barra da Tijuca and beyond p66
Barra da Tijuca offers a spectacular setting, but it's isolated and quite a trek from the centre.
$$$$ La Suite, R Jackson de Figueiredo, 501, Joá, T021-2484 1962, www.lasuiterio.com. Rio's only boutique hotel of distinction with 8 individually themed and exquisitely designed rooms perched like an eyrie over an exclusive beach in Rio's wealthiest small suburb. The rooms, the restaurant and the pool offer magical views. Pelé is a neighbour and the restaurant is run by Ludmila Soeiro, a former chef at one of Rio's best restaurants, **Zuka**.
$$ Rio Surf n Stay, R Raimundo Veras 1140, Recreio dos Bandeirantes, T021-3418 1133, www.riosurfnstay.com. Hostel and surf camp with double rooms, 6-bed dorms and camping. Free Wi-Fi. Surfing lessons and equipment rental are available.

✪ Restaurants

There are many restaurants in Rio but very few good ones. With the arrival of decent food from São Paulo in the 1990s things have been improving, especially in **Leblon**. But it is important not to be taken in by appearances or hotel concierges. Expect to pay at least US$30 per person in the better restaurants. At the cheaper end of the spectrum, Rio lacks that almost ubiquitous Brazilian institution, the corner bakery. Cariocas generally wolf down their breakfast and snacks on foot at streetside bars so a decent sit-down breakfast that isn't mock-French in appearance (and price) can be hard to find. But there are plenty of stand-up juice booths serving fruit juices made from as many as 25 different fruits from orange to *açai* and carrot to *cupuaçu*, all of which are wonderful. You can eat a filling lunch for an average US$5 per person, less if you choose the *prato feito* (US$1.50-6), or eat in a place that serves food by weight (starting at about US$10 per kg).

Central Rio and Lapa p32, map p30
Restaurants in the business district are generally only open for weekday lunch. Many *lanchonetes* in this area offer good cheap meals. The **Travessa do Comércio** has many extemporaneous street restaurants after 1800, especially on Fri, and is always buzzing with life. **R Miguel Couto** (opposite Santa Rita church) is called the 'Beco das Sardinhas'

because on Wed and Fri in particular it is full of people eating sardines and drinking beer.

There are several Arabic restaurants on **Av Senhor dos Passos**, which are also open Sat and Sun. In addition to those listed there are plenty of cafés, including a few chic new options on **R Lavradio** in Lapa, where the lively monthly Sat antiques market is held.

\$\$\$ Adega Flor de Coimbra, R Teotônio Regadas 34, Lapa, T021-2224 4582, www.adegaflordecoimbra. com.br. *Chope* and reliable Portuguese food, including excellent *bacalhau* and sardines in olive oil. Once the haunt of Carioca painter Cândido Portinari and Rio's left-wing intelligentsia.

\$\$\$ Eça, Av Rio Branco 128, T021-2524 2300, www.hstern.com.br/eca. Rio city centre's best business lunch from Frederic de Maeyer – a classically trained chef who once cooked in the Michelin-starred **L'Escalier du Palais Royale** in Brussels and who was *Gula* magazine's rising star chef in 2004.

\$\$\$ Republique, Praça da República 63, 2nd floor, Centro, T021-2532 9000. A long-established Rio favourite, now newly refurbished by the architect Chico Gouveia (whose decoration is based on the colours of the French flag), serving daring and ambitious South American fusion cooking by distinguished Rio chef Paulo Carvalho.

\$\$ Bar Luiz, R da Carioca 39, Centro, T021-2262 6900, www.barluiz.com.br. For 117 years this little bar in one of the few remaining colonial houses in the city centre has been at the heart of Rio life. Almost every Carioca you can name from Di Cavalcanti and Tom Jobim to Ronaldo and Chico Buarque has at one time or another formed part of the lively throng which gathers here on weekday evenings and most particularly on Fri and Sat to drink the famous *chope* and eat tapas.

\$\$ Café da Moda, Loja Folic, R Gonçalves Dias 49, 3rd floor, Centro, T021-2222 0610, www.folic.com.br. An a/c café devoted to the narrow waistline and located within the **Folic** shop. Salads are named after famous models.

\$\$-\$ Confeitaria Colombo, R Gonçalves Dias 32 (near Carioca *metrô* station), Centro, T021-2505 1500, www.confeitariacolombo.com.br. Afternoons only during the week. The only remaining belle-époque Portuguese coffee house in Rio, serving a range of café food, cakes, pastries and light lunches. The *feijoada colonial* on Sat is accompanied by live *choro*.

Santa Teresa *p47, map p48*

\$\$\$ Aprazível, R Aprazível 62, T021-2508 9174, www.aprazivel.com.br. Decent but unspectacular Brazilian dishes and seafood with one of the best restaurant views in the city: tables are outdoors in a tropical garden overlooking Guanabara Bay.

\$\$ Bar do Arnaudo, Largo do Guimarães, R Almte Alexandrino 316, T021-2252 7246. A modest-looking restaurant decorated with handicrafts but serving generous portions of wonderful northeast-Brazilian cooking. Try the *carne do sol* (sun-dried beef, or jerky) with *feijão de corda* (brown beans and herbs), or the *queijo coalho* (a country cheese, grilled).

$$ Espírito Santa, R Almte Alexandrino 264, T021-2507 4840. www.espiritosanta.com.br. Lunch only Tue, Wed, Sun; closed Mon. Upstairs is a chic boho restaurant with a view serving sumptuous Amazon food by Natacha Fink. Downstairs is a funky weekend basement club. Great cocktails.

$$ Portella, R Paschoal Carlos Magno 139/141, Largo do Guimarães, T021-2507 5181, www.portellabar.com.br. São Paulo-style corner restaurant-bar with good *picanha* steaks, award-winning *petiscos* (bar snacks). Try the *portadella* with flaky pastry stuffed with catupiry cream cheese and pistachio. Ice-cold *chopp*. Live music most weekend nights.

$$ Sobrenatural, R Almte Alexandrino 432, T021-2224 1003, www.restaurantesobrenatural.com. br. Simple, elegant seafood served by sexagenarian career waiters in bow ties. The huge dining room is always lively with chatter.

Botafogo and Urca *p53, map p54*
There are many cheap and mid-range options in the **Botafogo Praia** shopping centre.

$$$ Abençoado, Morro de Urca s/n, T021-2275 8925, www.abencoadorio. com.br. There can be few restaurants anywhere in the world with a better view than this: over the bay to Corcovado and the Christ on one side and the pearly Atlantic beaches of Copacabana, Ipanema and distant Niterói on the other. A menu of Brazilian comfort food given a gourmet twist. Plates include

angu (corn meal with Santa Catarina prawns and field mushrooms) or *escondidinho* (jerk meat with cheese gratin served on a bed of pureed aipim). The accompanying caipirinhas are the best in Rio.

$$$ Miam Miam, General Goes Monteiro 34, Botafogo, T021-2244 0125, www.miammiam.com.br. Closed Mon. The most fashionable of Rio's alternative fashion set sip caipirinhas here. Decoration is retro chic with 1950s and 1960s lounge furniture from the **Hully Gully** antique shop in Copacabana's Siqueira Campos mall and cartoons in homage to cult 1970s Carioca cartoonist, Carlos Zéfiro. Food is light Mediterranean.

$$$ Oui Oui, R Conde de Irajá, 85, T021-2527 3539, www.restaurante ouioui.com.br. Art deco lounge bar serving the *petiscos* (small plates of contemporary Brazilian food served tapas style and ordered in pairs) .

$$ Raajmahal, R General Polidoro 29, Baixo Botafogo, T021-2542 6242, www.raajmahal.com.br. One of the few restaurants in Brazil offering authentic Indian food with a huge menu including a range of vegetarian dishes such as *mater paneer*.

$$ Yorubá, R Arnaldo Quintela 94, Botafogo, T021-2541 9387, www. restauranteyoruba.com.br. Evenings only except weekends, closed Mon, Tue. Rio's favourite Bahian restaurant can be hard to find (there's nothing written on the building to indicate it's a restaurant), but it's well worth searching out. It has been voted the best in the city a number of times by *Veja* magazine. The menu comprises

Bahian and African food from *bobó de camarão* (prawn stew), *ewa* (fried, sliced fish with yam and dried prawns) and *acarajé* (beans fried in dendê palm oil) to *vatapá* (fish or chicken with coconut milk, shrimps, peanuts, dendê palm oil and chilli) alongside more unusual dishes such as chicken in ginger sauce with cashew nut rice.

Copacabana *p58, map p60*

There are stand-up bars selling snacks all around Copacabana and Ipanema. There are plenty of open-air restaurants along **Av Atlântica**, none of which can be recommended for anything but the view.

$$$ Cipriani, Copacabana Palace (see page 72). The best hotel restaurant for formal dining, with a chef from the **Hotel Cipriani** in Venice. Very good seafood and Italian fare.

$$$ Copa Café, Av Atlântica 3056, T021-2235 2947. A French bistro run by São Paulo chef Cássio Machado with light food and fabulous mini burgers with Dijon mustard. Very popular with Carioca celebrities like Caetano Veloso. DJ after dinner in the evenings at weekends.

$$$ La Fiorentina, Atlântica 458a, T021-2543 8395, www.lafiorentina. com.br. The Italian has been a Copa institution for over half a century and is famous for its *espaguete com frutos do mar* (seafood spaghetti), served in a light prawn marinade.

$$$ No Mangue, R Sá Ferreira 25 ljB, T021-2521 3237, www.nomangue. com.br. Copa's best northeast Brazilian and seafood restaurant offering sumptuous *moquecas*, *bobó*

de camarão and *petiscos* like crab or prawn pasty and squid in garlic oil.

$$$ Siri Mole and Cia, R Francisco Otaviano 90. Good Bahian seafood (and Italian coffee) in elegant a/c surroundings.

$$$-$$ Churrascaria Palace, R Rodolfo Dantas 16B, T021-2541 5898, www.churrascariapalace.com.br. Copa's answer to **Porção** or **Esplanada Grill** with 20 different kinds of barbecued meat served at your table with buffet salads to accompany.

$$-$ Aipo and Aipim, Av Nossa Senhora de Copacabana 391b and 920 in Copacabana, and R Visconde de Pirajá 145 in Ipanema, T021-2267 8313, www.aipoeaipim.com.br. Plentiful tasty food sold by weight at this popular chain.

$$-$ Eclipse, Av NS de Copacabana 1309, T021-2287 1788, www. bareclipse.com.br. Spruce, well-run and very popular 24-hr restaurant offering good-value *prato feito* lunches and a generous range of meats, pastas, snacks and sandwiches served in the cool interior or on streetside tables.

$ Cafeina, R Constante Ramos 44, T021-2547 8651, www.cafeina.biz. Very popular breakfast spot with good coffee, tasty pastries and other snacks and ice cold juices.

$ Cervantes, Barata Ribeiro 07-B at Prado Júnior 335B, T021 2275 6147, www.restaurantecervantes.com.br. Stand-up bar or sit-down a/c restaurant, open all night, queues after 2200. Said to serve the best sandwiches in town. A local institution.

$ Traiteurs de France, Av NS de Copacabana 386, T021 2548 6440.

Delicious French tarts and pastries, but poor service.

Ipanema and Leblon *p61, map p62*
$$$ Alessandro & Frederico, R Garcia D'Ávila151, Ipanema, T021-2522 5414, www.alessandroefrederico.com.br. Upmarket café with decent café latte and breakfasts.

$$$ Bistrô ZaZá, R Joana Angélica 40, Ipanema, T021-2247 9101, www.zazabistro.com.br. Hippy chic pseudo-Moroccan/French restaurant that attracts a mix of tourist and bohemian Zona Sul Cariocas.

$$$ Capricciosa, R Vinícius de Moraes 134, Ipanema, T021-2523 3394. The best pizzeria in town and a lynchpin in the TV and fashion scene – the famous and wealthy gather here to gossip and catch up. Queues can be long.

$$$ CT Boucherie, R Dias Ferreira 636, Leblon, T021-2529 2329, www.ctboucherie.com.br. Claude Troisgros, of **Olympe** expands his restaurant empire onto Leblon's gastronomic centre with this elegant, unpretentious meat restaurant. The focus is on the superb cuts of meat, accompanied by sauces of choice and delectable sides – honed to bring out the taste of the cuts of choice, and including English-inspired and tropically flavoured passion fruit infused pureed apple.

$$$ Esplanada Grill, R Barão da Torre 600, Ipanema, T021-2239 6028, www.esplanadagrill.com.br. The formal atmosphere and stiff penguin-suited staff aren't as much fun as the whirligig waiters at **Porção** but the meat can't be beat. Come here if you crave steak. There are no finer cuts in Rio.

$$$ Forneria, R Aníbal de Mendonça 112, Ipanema, T021-2540 8045, www.restauranteforneria.com.br. Paulistano restaurateur Rogerio Fasano's latest elegant eating-space in Rio serves supreme burgers in pizza dough and cooked in a wood-fired oven, and other superior bar snacks. Usually full with an elegant after-beach crowd.

$$$ Manekineko, R Dias Ferreira 410, Leblon, T021-2540 7641, www.manekineko.com.br. Rio's best Japanese with a large menu of superb traditional dishes and Japanese, European and South American fusion. The intimate dining area, comprising a corridor of low-lit booths, is always packed.

$$$ Porção, Barão de Torre 218, Ipanema, T021-3202 9158, www.porcao.com.br. One of the city's best *churrascarias* serving all manner of meat in unlimited quantities for a set price.

$$$ Satyricon, R Barão da Torre 192, Ipanema, T021-2521 0627, www.satyricon.com.br. The best seafood in Rio. Lively crowd in a large dining room which precludes intimacy. A favourite with businessmen, politicians and Ronaldo. Avoid Sat when there is a buffet.

$$$ Zuka, R Dias Ferreira 233B, Leblon, T021-3205 7154, www.zuka.com.br. Eclectic fusion of everything – French and Japanese, American fast food and Italian – all presented on huge rectangular plates and in a carefully designed modern space.

\$\$ Big Nectar, R Teixeira de Melo 34, T021-2522 3949. One of the largest range of juices in Rio including uniquely South American and Brazilian fruits such as *seriguela*, *mangaba*, *umbu* and *cupuaçu*.

\$\$ Casa da Feijoada, Prudente de Morais 10, Ipanema, T021-2247 2776. Excellent *feijoada* all week. Generous portions.

\$\$ Celeiro, R Dias Ferreira 199, Leblon, T021-2274 7843, www.celeiroculinaria. com.br. Superior salads and buffet food, which has been consistently voted the best in the city by the magazine, *Veja*.

\$\$ Fellini, R General Urquiza 104, Leblon, T021-2511 3600, www. fellini.com.br. The best pay-by-weight restaurant in the city with a large range of delicious Brazilian and international dishes, salads and quiches. Plenty of options for vegetarians. Funky website.

\$\$ Polis Sucos, R Maria Quitéria 70a, T021-2247 2518. A favourite Carioca pre- and post-beach pit-stop offering a huge range of tropical juices and snacks such as *açai na tigela* (mushed *açai* berries with *guarana* syrup).

Gávea, Lagoa and Jardim Botânico *p64, map p62*

Gávea is the heartland of trendy 20-something Rio. The neighbourhoods of Jardim Botânico and Lagoa appear at first sight to offer unlimited exciting upmarket dining opportunities, but the restaurants are mostly mutton dressed up as lamb. They look great, cost loads and serve dreadful food. The following are the few exceptions.

\$\$\$ Olympe, R Custódio Serrão 62, Lagoa, T021-2539 4542, www. claudetroisgros. com.br. The Troisgros family were founders of nouvelle cuisine and run a 3 Michelin-star restaurant in Roanne. Claude Troisgros' cooking fuses tropical ingredients with French techniques, exemplified by the roasted quail filled with *farofa* and served with raisins, pearl onions and a sweet and sour *jabuticaba* sauce.

\$\$\$ Roberta Sudbrack, R Lineu de Paula Machado 916, Jardim Botânico, T021-3874 0139, www.roberta sudbrack.com.br. Roberta was the private chef for President Henrique Cardoso and cooked for all the visiting international dignitaries who dined with him during his term of office. She is celebrated for her European-Brazilian fusion cooking and won *Veja*'s coveted chef-of-the-year award in 2006.

🎵 Bars and clubs

Rio nightlife is young and vivacious. **Lapa** is a current hotspot at weekends, once down-at-heel and still not entirely safe but undergoing a great renaissance, with a string of clubs along **Mem de Sá** and **R Lavradio** and along a little back street known as the **Beco do Rato**. The whole neighbourhood throbs to dance rhythms from samba and *forró* to techno and hip-hop. Similarly busy, even on Sun and Mon, is **Baixa Gávea**, where beautiful 20-somethings gather around Praça Santos Dumont.

Wherever you are in Rio, there's a bar near you. Beer costs around US\$2.50 for a large bottle, but up to

US$7 in the plusher venues, where you are often given a card that includes 2 drinks and a token entrance fee. A cover of US$3-7 may be charged made for live music, or there might be a minimum consumption charge of around US$3, sometimes both. Snack food is always available. **Copacabana**, **Ipanema** and **Leblon** have many beach *barracas*, several open all night. The seafront bars on Av Atlântica are great for people-watching, but avoid those towards **Leme** as some may offer more than beer.

Clubs on and around Rio's beaches are generally either fake Europe, eg **Melt** and **Bunker** (although decent DJs like Marky play here), or fake US, eg **Nuth** and **00**. Santa Teresa has the most interesting bohemian bars and is a good place to begin a weekend night before heading down the hill to Lapa, Rio's capital of nightlife, with a plethora of samba venues undergoing a steady renaissance. See also Samba schools, page 86.

Central Rio, Lapa and Santa Teresa *p32 and p47, maps p30 and p48*

Lapa, Santa Teresa and increasingly, the city centre, have Rio's most interesting, bohemian nightlife and shouldn't be missed if you are in Rio over a weekend. Ideally come early on a Sat for the afternoon market and live street tango on **R Lavradio**, eat in Santa Teresa and sample the bars on the **Largo dos Guimarães** and the **Largo das Neves** before returning to Lapa for live samba or funk. Although it is easy to walk between the 2 *bairros*, never walk alone and always be wary of pickpockets.

Bar do Mineiro, R Paschoal Carlos Magno 99, 100 m from Largo dos Guimarães, Santa Teresa, T021-2221 9227. Rustic *boteco* opening right onto the street and with hundreds of black-and-white photos of Brazilian musicians displayed on the white-tiled walls. Attracts a busy, arty young crowd.

Carioca da Gema, Av Mem de Sá 79, Centro, near **Rio Scenarium**, T021-2221 0043, www.barcariocadagema. com.br. One of the longest established samba clubs and daytime cafés in Lapa, with the cream of the live bands and, if you arrive early, sit-down tables. Great little pre-show pizza restaurant upstairs.

Circo Voador, see Live music, page 84. One of the best venues in Rio.

Club Six, R das Marrecas 38, Lapa, T021 2510 3230, www.clubsix.com.br. Huge pounding European/NYC dance club with everything from hip-hop to ambient house.

Clube dos Democráticos, R do Riachuelo 91, A grungy old dance hall where transvestites gossip on the stairs and bands play Gafieira or dance hall samba.

Espírito Santa, R Almte Alexandrino 264, Largo do Guimarães, Santa Teresa, T021-2508 7095, www.espiritosanta. com.br. Upstairs restaurant, downstairs lively club where every Sat DJ Zod plays the best in Rio funk and West African dance.

Estudantina Musical, 3 piso, Praça Tiradentes 79, T021-2232 1149. Closed Mon-Wed. This is one of central Rio's most famous old school gafieira halls. It's at its busiest and liveliest on Thu when hundreds gather to dance samba to some of the best big samba bands in the city. Far less touristy than Lapa.

Rio Scenarium, R do Lavradio 20, Lapa, T021-3147 9005, www.rioscenarium. com.br. 3-storey samba and dance club in a beguilingly spacious colonial house used as a movie prop storage facility by *TV Globo*. Overflowing with Brazilian exuberance and people of all ages dancing furiously, to samba and assorted Euro and Lusitanian club sounds, and the bizarre backdrop of a 19th-century apothecary's shop or mannequins wearing 1920s outfits. Arrive after 2300.

Sacrilégio, Av Mem de Sá 81, Lapa, next door to **Carioca da Gema**, T021-3970 1461, www.sacrilegio. com.br. Samba, *chorinho*, *pagode* and occasional theatre. Close to many other bars.

Semente, R Joaquim Silva 138, Lapa, T021-2242 5165. Mon-Sat from 2200, US$8 cover, minimum consumption US$7. Popular for samba, *choro* and salsa. Book at weekends. Great atmosphere. Recommended.

The Week, R Sacadura Cabral 154, Zona Portuária, T021-2253 1020, www.theweek.com.br. One of the most popular dance clubs in the city, with a mostly gay crowd and with state-of-the-art dance spaces, and New York house and Eurotrash here.

Botafogo and Urca *p53, map p54*
Casa da Matriz, R Henrique de Novaes 107, Botafogo, T021-2226 9691, www.matrizonline.com.br. Great

grungy club with a bar, Atari room, small cinema and 2 dance floors. Full of Rio students.

Copacabana, Ipanema and Leblon *p58 and p60, maps p60 and p62*
There is frequent live music on the beaches of Copacabana and Ipanema, and along the **Av Atlântica** throughout the summer, especially around New Year.

Academia da Cachaça, R Conde de Bernadotte 26-G, Leblon, T021-2529 2680, with another branch at Av Armando Lombardi 800, Barra da Tijuca, www.academiadacachaca.com. br. The best *cachacas* and caipirinhas in the city (try the delicious *pitanga* caipirinha), and some of Rio's best *feijoadas* and bar snacks. Good on Fri.

Bar do Copa, **Hotel Copacabana Palace**, Av Atlântica 1702, T021-2545 8724. This mock-Miami beach cocktail bar next to the pool at the swish **Copacabana Palace** hotel is a favourite high society posing spot and is much frequented by models and celebrities. Dress well to get past the velvet rope, and be prepared to queue.

Barril 1800, Av Vieira Souto 110, Ipanema, T021-2523 0085, www. barril1800.com. Pleasant place to watch the sunset with a cold glass of *chope* beer in hand.

Clandestino, R Barata Ribeiro 111, T021-3798 5771, www.clandestinobar. com.br. A cavernous little cellar bar attracting a lively young crowd who dance to soul, Rio funk and occasional live acts. Busiest on Fri.

Devassa, R Rainha Guilhermina 48, Leblon, and an alternative menu at Ipanema branch, Av Visconde de Pirajá 539, www.devassa. com.br/cervejaria. php. A 2-floor pub-bar-restaurant that is always heaving with the Ipanema middle class. Brews its own beer.

Empório, R Maria Quitéria 37, Ipanema, T021-3813 2526. Street bar that attracts the hordes. Mon is the busiest night.

Garota de Ipanema, R Vinícius de Moraes 49, Ipanema. Where the song *Girl from Ipanema* was written. Now packed with foreigners on the package Rio circuit listening to bossa. For the real thing head to **Toca do Vinícius** on a Sun afternoon (see page 84).

Melt, R Rita Ludolf 47, Leblon, T021-2249 9309, www.melt-rio.com.br. Downstairs bar and upstairs sweaty club. Occasional performances by the cream of Rio's new samba funk scene, usually on a Sun. Always heaving on Thu.

Shenanigans, R Visconde de Pirajá 112, Ipanema, T021-2267 5860, www.shenanigans.com.br. Obligatory mock-Irish bar with Guinness and Newcastle Brown. Not a place to mix with the locals.

Vinícius, R Vinícius de Moraes 39, Ipanema, www.viniciusbar.com.br. Mirror image of the **Garota de Ipanema** with slightly better acts and food.

Gávea, Lagoa and Jardim Botânico *p64, map p62*

00 (Zero Zero), Av Padre Leonel Franca 240, Gávea, T021-2540 8041, www.00site.com.br. Mock-LA bar/restaurant/club with a small outdoor area. Currently the trendiest club in

Rio for Brazil's equivalent of 'sloanes' or 'valley girls'. Gay night on Sun.

Bar Lagoa, Av Epitácio Pessoa 1674, Lagoa, T021-2523 1135, www.bar lagoa.com.br. Attracts an older arty crowd on weekdays.

Hipódromo da Gávea, Praça Santos Dumont 108, Gávea, T021-2274 9720. On weekend and Thu nights this restaurant bar, and its neighbours, fill with young middle-class Cariocas who talk and flirt over beer and bar snacks. The crowds from all bars spill out onto Praça Santos Dumont square. Very few tourists make it here.

Barra da Tijuca *p66*

Nuth, R Armando Lombardi 999, www.nuth.com.br. Barra's slickest club; very mock-Miami and frequented by a mixed crowd of rich-kid surfers, footballers (including Romario) and women with surgically enhanced beauty.

⊕ Entertainment

Rio de Janeiro *p22, maps p24, p30, p33, p48, p52, p54, p60 and p62*
Cinema
There are cinemas serving subtitled Hollywood fare and major Brazilian releases on the top floor of almost all the malls.

Live music
Cariocas congregate in Lapa between Thu and Sat for live club music. There are free concerts throughout the summer along the Copacabana and Ipanema beaches, in Botafogo and at the parks: mostly samba, reggae, rock

Pedro Luís e A Parede recommends

Pedro Luís and his band play some of the most exciting new samba in Rio, integrating the style with other Brazilian rhythms, modern electronica and indie. They play live in Rio regularly and you can check them out on www.plap.com.br. Here are Pedro's recommendations for what to do in Rio: Circo Voador, www.circovoador.com.br and Fundição Progresso, T021-2220 5070, www.fundicao.org, are arts and music centres with concert halls, where some of the city's most exciting new performers and film-makers showcase their talents. The Circo runs a lot of social projects too and is in a beautiful location beneath the Arcos de Lapa. The Espaço Cultural Municipal Sérgio Porto, Rua Humaitá 163, Humaitá, T021-2266 0896, is another arts space with two galleries and a theatre where you can see everything from live music to alternative poetry or performance art – all from some of the freshest and most innovative performers in the city.

and MPB (Brazilian pop). There is no advance schedule; information is given in the local press. Rio's famous jazz, in all its forms, is performed in lots of enjoyable venues too, see www.samba-choro.com.br for more information.
Centro Cultural Carioca, R do Teatro 37, T021-2242 9642, www.centroculturalcarioca.com.br. Open 1830-late. This restored old house with wraparound balconies and exposed brick walls is a dance school and music venue that attracts a lovely mix of people. Professional dancers perform with musicians; after a few tunes the audience joins in. Thu is impossibly crowded; Sat is calmer. Bar food available. US$12 cover charge. Highly recommended.
Circo Voador, R dos Arcos, Lapa, T021-2533 0354, www.circovoador.com.br. Lapa's recuperation began with this little concert hall under the arches.

Some of the city's best smaller acts still play here – including Seu Jorge who first found fame playing with *Farofa Carioca* at the Circo.
Rhapsody, Av Epitácio Pessoa 1104, Lagoa, T021-2247 2104, http://rhapsodypianobar.sites.uol.com.br. Piano-bar restaurant with a mix of Brazilian and Diana Kraal-style crooning.
Toca do Vinícius, R Vinícius de Moraes 129C, Ipanema, www.tocadovinicius.com.br. Rio's leading bossa nova and *choro* record shop has concerts from some of the finest performers every Sun lunchtime.

Theatre
There are about 40 theatres in Rio, presenting a variety of classical and modern performances in Portuguese. For information check on the website www.rioecultura.com.br.

SESC cultural centres

Little known to visitors but beloved of cultured Brazilians are the SESC centres. These are spaces devoted to arts in general, with fine art and photographic exhibitions, theatre, film and, in the **Espaço SESC** in Copacabana, live music. Many established highbrow contemporary artists like Naná Vasconcelos and Egberto Gismonti have played here. There are several SESC centres in Rio and the excellent website www. sescrj.com.br (in Portuguese only but easy to follow) has information on forthcoming concerts.
Espaço SESC, Rua Domingos Ferreira 160, Copacabana, T021-2547 0156.
SESC Tijuca, Rua Barão de Mesquita 539, Barra da Tijuca, T021-3238 2100.
SESC Niterói, Rua Padre Anchieta 56, Niterói, T021-2719 9119.

✪ Festivals

Rio de Janeiro *p22, maps p24, p30, p33, p48, p52, p54, p60 and p62*
Carnaval
Tickets → *See also box, page 88.*
Sambódromo, R Marquês de Sapucaí s/n, Cidade Nova. http://carnaval.rio guiaoficial.com.br and www.rioguia oficial.com.br. The nearest tube is Praça Onze.

The Sambódromo parades start at 1900 and last about 12 hrs. Gates open at 1800. There are *cadeiras* (seats) at ground level, *arquibancadas* (terraces) and *camarotes* (boxes). The best boxes are reserved for tourists and VIPs and are very expensive or by invitation only. Seats are closest to the parade, but you may have to fight your way to the front. Sectors 4, 7 and 11 are the best spots (they house the judging points); 6 and 13 are least favoured (being at the end when dancers might be tired) but have more space. The terraces, while uncomfortable, house the most fervent fans and are tightly packed; this is the best place to soak up the atmosphere but it's too crowded to take pictures. Tickets start at US$100 for *arquibancadas* and are sold at travel agencies as well as the Maracanã Stadium box office (see page 45). Travel agency: **Carnaval Turismo**, Av Nossa Senhora de Copacabana 583, T021-2548 4232, www.carnavalinrio.com.br. Tickets should be bought as far as possible in advance; they are usually sold out before Carnaval weekend but touts outside can often sell you tickets at inflated prices. Samba schools have an allocation of tickets which members sometimes sell, if you are offered one of these check the date. Tickets for the champions' parade on the Sat following Carnaval are much cheaper. Many tour companies offer Rio trips including Carnaval, but tickets are at inflated prices.

Sleeping and security
Be sure to reserve accommodation well in advance. Virtually all hotels raise their prices during Carnaval,

although it is usually possible to find a reasonably priced room. Your property should be safe inside the Sambódromo, but the crowds outside can attract pickpockets; as ever, don't brandish your camera, and only take the money you need for fares and refreshments (food and drink are sold in the Sambódromo). It gets hot, so wear shorts and a T-shirt.

Taking part

Most samba schools will accept a number of foreigners and you will be charged from US$175 up to US$435 for your costume depending on which school of samba you choose. This money helps to fund poorer members of the school. You should be in Rio for at least 2 weeks before Carnaval. It is essential to attend fittings and rehearsals on time, to show respect for your section leaders and to enter into the competitive spirit of the event. For those with the energy and the dedication, it will be an unforgettable experience.

Rehearsals

Ensaios are held at the schools' *quadras* from Oct onwards and are well worth seeing. It is wise to go by taxi, as most schools are based in poorer districts.

Carnaval shows

Tour agents sell tickets for glitzy samba shows, which are nothing like the real thing. When buying a Carnaval DVD, make sure the format is compatible (NTSC for USA or most of Europe; PAL for the UK, region 4).

Carnival dates

→ **2015** 13-18 February
→ **2016** 5-10 February
→ **2017** 24 February-1 March

Samba school addresses and parties

Samba schools hold parties throughout the year, especially at the weekends. These are well worth visiting. See websites for details.
Acadêmicos de Salgueiro, R Silva Teles 104, Andaraí, T021-2238 5564, www.salgueiro.com.br.
Beija Flor de Nilópolis, Pracinha Wallace Paes Leme 1025, Nilópolis, T021-2791 2866, www.beija-flor.com.br.
Imperatriz Leopoldinense, R Prof Lacê 235, Ramos, T021-2560 8037, www.imperatrizleopoldinense.com.br.
Mocidade Independente de Padre Miguel, R Coronel Tamarindo 38, Padre Miguel, T021-3332 5823, www.mocidadeindependente.com.br.
Portela, R Clara Nunes 81, Madureira, T021-2489 6440, www.gresportela.com.br.
Primeira Estação de Mangueira, R Visconde de Niterói 1072, Mangueira, T021-2567 4637, www.mangueira.com.br.
Unidos da Viradouro, Av do Contorno 16, Niterói, T021-2516 1301, www.gresuviradouro.com.br.
Vila Isabel, Boulevard 28 de Setembro, Vila Isabel, T021-2578 0077, www.gresunidosdevilaisabel.com.br.

Transport

Taxis to the Sambódromo are negotiable and will find your gate, the nearest *metrô* is Praça Onze and this can be an enjoyable ride in the company of costumed samba school members. You can follow the participants to the *concentração*, the assembly and formation on Av Presidente Vargas, and mingle with them while they queue to enter the Sambódromo. Ask if you can take photos.

Useful information

Carnaval week comprises an enormous range of official and unofficial contests and events, which reach a peak on the Tue. **Riotur**'s guide booklet and website gives concise information on these in English. The entertainment sections of newspapers and magazines such as *O Globo*, *Jornal do Brasil*, *Manchete* and *Veja Rio* are worth checking. Felipe Ferreira's guide to the Rio Carnaval, *Liga Independente das Escolas de Samba do Rio de Janeiro*, www.liesa.com.br, has good explanations of the competition, rules, the schools, a map and other practical details.

Other festivals

20 Jan The **festival of São Sebastião**, patron saint of Rio, is celebrated by an evening procession, leaving Capuchinhos church in Tijuca and arriving at the cathedral of São Sebastião. On the same evening, an *umbanda* festival is celebrated at the *Caboclo* monument in Santa Teresa.
Jun The **Festas Juninas** are celebrated throughout Brazil. In Rio they start with the **Festival of Santo Antônio** on 13 Jun, when the main event is a Mass, followed by celebrations at the Convento do Santo Antônio and the Largo da Carioca. All over the state, the **Festival of São João** is a major event, marked by huge bonfires on the night of 23-24 Jun. It is traditional to dance the *quadrilha* and drink *quentão*, *cachaça* and sugar, spiced with ginger and cinnamon, served hot. The Festas Juninas close with the **Festival of São Pedro** on 29 Jun. Being the patron saint of fishermen, his feast is normally accompanied by processions of boats.
Oct This is the month of the feast of **Nossa Senhora da Penha** (see page 45).
30 Dec Less hectic than Carnaval, but very atmospheric, is the **Festival of Yemanjá** when devotees of the *orixá* of the sea dress in white and gather at night on Copacabana, Ipanema and Leblon beaches, singing and dancing around open fires and making offerings. The elected Queen of the Sea is rowed along the seashore. At midnight small boats are launched as offerings to Yemanjá. The religious event is dwarfed, however, by a massive New Year's Eve party, called **Reveillon** at Copacabana. The beach is packed as thousands of revellers enjoy free outdoor concerts by big-name pop stars, topped with a lavish midnight firework display. It is most crowded in front of the Copacabana Palace Hotel. Another good place to see the fireworks is at the far end of the beach in front of R Princesa Isabel, famous for its fireworks waterfall at about 0010. Many followers of Yemanjá now make offerings on 29 or 30 Dec and at Barra da Tijuca or Recreio dos Bandeirantes to avoid the crowds and noise of Reveillon.

Carnaval

Carnaval in Rio is as spectacular as its reputation suggests – a riot of colour, flamboyance and artistry unrivalled outside Brazil. On the Friday before Shrove Tuesday, the mayor of Rio hands the keys of the city to *Rei Momo*, the Lord of Misrule, signifying the start of a five-day party. Imagination runs riot, social barriers are broken and the main avenues, full of people and children wearing fancy dress, are colourfully lit. Areas throughout the city such as the Terreirão de Samba in Praça Onze are used for shows, music and dancing. Spectacularly dressed carnival groups throng around the Sambódromo (Oscar Niemeyer's purpose-built stadium, see page 44) strutting, drumming and singing in preparation for their parade. And there are *blocos* (parades) throughout the city, in neighbourhoods such as Santa Teresa and Ipanema. It can be ghostly quiet in the southern beach zones during this time.

Unlike Salvador, which remains a wild street party, Rio's Carnaval is a designated parade, taking place over a number of days and contained within the Sambódromo stadium. Alongside the parade are a number of *bailes* (parties) held within designated clubs, street shows like those held around Praça Onze.

There are numerous samba schools in Rio, which are divided into two leagues before they parade through the Sambódromo. The 14 schools of the *Grupo Especial* parade on Sunday and Monday while the *Grupos de Acesso* A and B parade on Saturday and Friday respectively. There is also a *mirins* parade (younger members of the established schools) on Tuesday. Judging takes place on Wednesday afternoon and the winners of the groups parade again on the following Saturday. Tickets to these winners' parades are always easy to get hold of even when all others are sold out.

Every school comprises 2500-6000 participants divided into *alas* (wings) each with a different costume and parading on or around five to nine *carros alegóricos* (beautifully designed floats). Each school chooses an *enredo* (theme) and composes a samba that is a poetic, rhythmic and catchy expression of the theme. The *enredo* is further developed through the design of the floats and costumes. A *bateria* (percussion wing) maintains a reverberating beat that must keep the entire school, and the audience, dancing throughout the parade. Each procession follows a set order with the first to appear being the *comissão de frente* (a choreographed group that presents the school and the theme to the public). Next comes the *abre alas* (a magnificent float usually bearing the name or symbol of the school). The *alas* and other floats follow as well as *porta bandeiras* (flag bearers) and *mestre salas* (couples dressed in 18th-century costumes bearing the school's flag), and *passistas* (groups traditionally of mulata dancers). An *ala of baianas* (elderly women with circular skirts that swirl as they dance) is always included as is the *velha guarda* (distinguished members of the school) who close the parade. Schools are given between 65 and 80 minutes and lose points for failing to keep within this time. Judges award points to each school for components of their procession, such as costume, music and design, and make deductions for lack of energy, enthusiasm or discipline. The winners of the *Grupos de Acesso* are promoted to the next higher group while the losers, including those of the *Grupo Especial*, are relegated to the next lowest group. Competition is intense and the winners gain a monetary prize funded by the entrance fees.

The Carnaval parades are the culmination of months of intense activity by community groups, mostly in the city's poorest districts. Rio's *bailes* (fancy-dress balls) range from the sophisticated to the wild. The majority of clubs and hotels host at least one. The **Copacabana Palace**'s is elegant and expensive whilst the **Scala** club has licentious parties. It is not necessary to wear fancy dress; just join in, although you will feel more comfortable if you wear a minimum of clothing to the clubs, which are crowded, hot and rowdy. The most famous are the **Red and Black Ball** (Friday) and the **Gay Ball** (Tuesday) which are both televized. Venues for these vary.

Bandas and *blocos* can be found in all neighbourhoods and some of the most popular and entertaining are: **Cordão do Bola Preta** (meets at 0900 on Saturday, Rua 13 de Maio 13, Centro); **Simpatia é Quase Amor** (meets at 1600 on Sunday, Praça General Osório, Ipanema) and the transvestite **Banda da Ipanema** (meets at 1600 on Saturday and Tuesday, Praça General Osorio, Ipanema). It is necessary to join a *bloco* in advance to receive their distinctive T-shirts, but anyone can join in with the *bandas*. The expensive hotels offer special Carnaval breakfasts from 0530. **Caesar Park** is highly recommended for a wonderful meal and a top-floor view of the sunrise over the beach.

Rio de Janeiro *p22, maps p24, p30, p33, p48, p52, p54, p60 and p62*

Arts and crafts

La Vereda, R Almirante Alexandrino 428, Santa Teresa, T021-2507 0317, www.lavereda.art.br. Colourful arty little boutique filled with crafts, from illuminated *favela* models to textiles, toys and paintings.

Novo Desenho (**ND**), Av Infante Dom Henrique 85, Glória (next to MAM), T021-2524 2290, www.novodesenho. com.br. This pocket-sized boutique stocks a range of homeware and furniture from some of Brazil's best small artisan designers. These include established names such as Sergio Rodrigues (whose Mole chair is in MoMa New York's permanent collection) and Mendes-Hirth (who won an award at the 2010 iF Product Design Awards in Germany) alongside up-and-coming designers like Morito Ebine, whose chairs are built entirely of Brazilian wood with hardwood pins instead of screws. Many of the items are small enough to fit in a suitcase.

Fashion

Fashion is one of the best buys in Brazil, with a wealth of Brazilian designers selling clothes of the same quality as European or US famous names at a fraction of the price. Rio is the best place in the world for buying high-fashion bikinis. The best shops in Ipanema are in the **Forum de Ipanema** arcade, R Visconde de Pirajá 351 (where you will find many of the best beachwear brands), **Garcia D'Ávila** and **R Nascimento Silva**, which runs off it. The latter areas are home to some of the best Brazilian designers, together with international big-name stalwarts like Louis Vuitton and Cartier, and Brazil's classiest jeweller, Antonio Bernardo. Most of the international names, together with all the big Brazilian names are also housed in the **São Conrado Fashion Mall**.

There are some little shops on **Aires Saldanha**, Copacabana (1 block back from beach), which are good for bikinis and cheaper than in the shopping centres. For good-value shopping head for **SAARA**, www.saararario.com.br, a complex of some 600 shops in the city centre covering several blocks between R Alfandega, R dos Andradas, Praça da Republica and R Buenos Aires where you will find bargain-basement clothing, costume jewellery, toys, perfume and sundry items.

Blue Man, R Visconde de Pirajá, 351, lojas C & D, T021-2247 4905, also at São Conrado Fashion Mall. Tiny, bright bikinis beloved of those with perfect bodies.

Bum Bum, R Visconde de Pirajá 351, Ipanema, T021-2287 9951, www. bumbum.com.br. Together with **Rosa Cha**, one of the most internationally renowned bikini designers, tiny and beautifully cut.

Carlos Tufvesson, R Nascimento Silva 304, Ipanema, T021-2523 9200, www.carlostufvesson.com. Sensual evening wear in high-quality fabric.

Casa Turuna, R Senhor dos Passos 77, T021-2509 3908, www.casaturuna. com.br. The place to buy your Carnaval costumes in or out of carnival season, together with samba skirts, masks and general pageantry. Open since 1915.

Lenny, R Visconde de Pirajá, 351, Ipanema, T021-2287 9951, and in the **São Conrado Fashion Mall**. Lenny Niemeyer is widely regarded as Brazil's most sophisticated bikini designer.

Maria Bonita, R Visconde de Praiaja 351, lj 109 & R Aníbal de Mendonça 135, Ipanema, T021-2540 5354, www.mariabonitaextra.com.br. Impeccably cut, elegantly simple, sophisticated women's wear in high-quality fabrics.

Oh Boy!, R Visconde de Pirajá 550, Ipanema, T021-3875 7231, www.ohboy.com.br. Brightly coloured beach and casual wear for teens and 20-somethings. Very à la mode with big spreads in recent editions of Brazilian *Vogue*.

Osklen, R Maria Quitéria 85, Ipanema, T021-2227 2911, www.osklen.com. Elegant, casual-chic men's wear from a label which has been described as Brazil's answer to Ralph Lauren.

Salinas, R Visconde de Pirajá 547 & 351, lj 20 Ipanema, T021-2274 0644, and fashion mall, T021-2422 0677. Very highly regarded Brazilian bikinis: small, exquisitely made with great attention to detail and using only the best fabrics, in a variety of contemporary styles from hand crochet and beading to reversibles in multiple colour combinations.

Football souvenirs

Loja Fla, Av Nossa Senhora de Copacabana 219C, T021-2295 5057, www.lojafla.com.br. All things related to Brazil's favourite team, Flamengo,
from rare and limited edition kit to, balls, boots, DVDs and memorabilia.

Jewellery

Only buy precious and semi-precious stones from reputable dealers. There are several good jewellery shops at the Leme end of Av NS de Copacabana and branches of big international Brazilian names **Stern** and **Amsterdam Sauer** in Ipanema. **Antônio Bernado**, R Garcia d'Ávila 121, Ipanema, T021-2512 7204, and in the **São Conrado Fashion Mall**. Brazil's foremost jeweller who has been making beautifully understated pieces with contemporary designs for nearly 30 years. Internationally well known but available only in Brazil.

Markets

The **northeastern market** takes place at the Centro Luiz Gonzaga de Tradições Nordestinas, Campo de São Cristóvão, www.feiradesaocristovao.org.br, with music and magic, on Fri from 1800, Sat 0800-2200 and Sun 0800-1200 (bus No 472 or 474 from Copacabana or centre). There's a Sat **antiques market** on the waterfront near Praça 15 de Novembro, 1000-1700. Also on Praça 15 de Novembro is **Feirarte II**, Thu and Fri 0800-1800. **Feirarte I** is an open-air handicrafts market (everyone calls it the **Feira Hippy**) at Praça Gen Osório, Ipanema, www.feirahippieipanema.com, Sun 0700-1900; touristy but fun, with items from all over Brazil. **Babilônia Feira Hype** is held every other weekend at the Jockey Club 1400-2300. This lively and popular market has lots of stalls selling clothes and crafts, as well as massage and live music and dance performances. A **stamp and coin market** is held on Sun in the Passeio Público. There are **markets** on Wed 0700-1300 on R Domingos Ferreira and on Thu, same hours, on Praça do Lido, both Copacabana. Praça do Lido also has a **Feir Arte** on weekends 0800-1800. There is an **artesania market** nightly by the Othon Hotel, near R Miguel Lemos: one part for paintings, one part for everything else. There's a **Sunday market** on R da Glória, selling colourful, cheap fruit, vegetables and flowers; and an early morning **food market**, 0600-1100, R Min Viveiros de Castro, Ipanema. An excellent **food and household goods markets** take place at various places in the city and suburbs (see newspapers for times and places). **Feira do Livro** is a book market that moves around various locations (Largo do Machado, Cinelândia, Nossa Senhora da Paz, Ipanema), selling books at 20% discount.

Music

Arlequim Música, Paço Imperial, Praça XV de Novembro 48, loja 1, T021-2220 8471, www.arlequim.com. br. Mon-Fri 1000-2000 Sat 1000-1800. A good selection of high-quality Brazilian music and film.
Bossa Nova e Companhia, R Duvivier 37a, T021-2295 8096, www.bossanova ecompanhia.com.br. This long-established music shop, with its chic dragon's-tooth paving, has a little music museum in the basement and the best selection of bossa nova, *chorinho* and Brazilian jazz in the

city. The shop is next to the Beco das Garrafas alley, where Tom Jobim and João Gilberto first played together, **Toca do Vinícius**, R Vinícius de Moraes 129C, Ipanema, T021-2247 5227, www.tocadovinicius.com. br. Specializes in bossa nova books, CDs and souvenirs, doubles as a performance space.

Shopping centres

Rio Sul, at the Botafogo end of Túnel Novo, www.riosul.com.br.
Shopping Leblon, Av Afrânio de Melo Franco 290, www.shoppingleblon. com.br. The most fashionable mall in the Zona Sul. After the **São Conrado Fashion Mall**, it's the best one-stop shopping mall for Rio's most sought-after labels, less than 5 mins' walk from the beach.
Shopping Village Mall, Av das Americas 3900, Barra da Tijuca, T021-3252 2999, www.shoppingvillagemall. com.br. This vast mega-shopping mall opened in 2012 to much fanfare. It's packed with big name Brazilian and international brands, including the first **Apple** store in the country.

Other shopping centres, which have a wide variety of shops and services, include: **São Conrado Fashion Mall**, Estrada da Gavea 899, T021-2111 4444, www.scfashionmall.com.br; **Shopping Cidade Copacabana**, R Siqueira Campos, www.shoppingcidade copacabana.com.br; **Shopping Botafogo Praia**, Praia de Botafogo 400, T021-3171 9559, www.botafogopraia shopping.com.br; **Norte Shopping** (Todos os Santos); **Plaza Shopping** (Niterói); and **Barra** in Barra da Tijuca.

⬤ What to do

Rio de Janeiro *p22, maps p24, p30, p33, p48, p52, p54, p60 and p62*
Boat trips
Several companies offer trips to **Ilha de Paquetá**, and day cruises, including lunch, to **Jaguanum Island**, and a sundown cruise around **Guanabara Bay**.

Moreno Urca, Quadrado de Urca, T021-9316 6733, www.morenourca. blogspot.com. Great low-key boat tours of the bay and Atlantic in a fisherman's wooden boat, calling at some of the less-visited sights such as Adam and Eve beach in Jurujuba, the Cagarras islands (for snorkelling) and the Forte São João. Book ahead in high season as it's a little boat. Bring sun protection.

Pink Fleet, Av Infante Dom Henrique s/n loja 2, Flamengo, T021-2555 4063, www.pinkfleet.com.br. Bay and ocean cruises in a very comfortable big iron cruiser, the Spirit of Brazil. Restaurants, bars and plenty of shade on board.

Saveiros Tour, Av Infante Dom Henrique s/n lojas 13 & 14, T021-2225 6064, www.saveiros.com.br. Tours in sailing schooners around the bay and down the coast, Mon-Fri 0900-1730, Sat and Sun 0900-1200. Also 'Baía da Guanabara Histórica' historical tours.

Driving tours and personal drivers
Andre Albuquerque, T021-7811 2737/2427 3629, andrealbuquerque@ yahoo.com.br. Private driver tours of Rio from a genuine 'Carioca da Gema'

(born and bred local). Friendly, reliable, helpful with English-speaking guides on request.

Madson Araujo, T021-9395 3537, www.tourguiderio.com. Bespoke personal tours of the Rio city sights and trips into Rio de Janeiro state.

Otávio Monteiro, T021-8835 1160 or T021-7841 4799, om2brasil@hotmail. com. Good-value driver and personal tours will go anywhere in Rio or the state. Reliable, good English.

Roz Brazil, T024-9257 0236, www.rozbrazil. com. Some of the best tours around Petrópolis, Teresópolis and the Serra dos Órgãos with British Brazilian Rosa Thompson, who has been living in the area for decades. Pick-ups from Rio.

Football coaching
Pelé da Praia, R Garcia D'Avila, Ipanema, T021-9702 5794, www. peledapraia.com. Football and volleyball coaching from a real Carioca character who has been working on Ipanema beach for many years.

Hang-gliding and paragliding
Delta Flight, T021-3322 5750, T021-9693 8800, www.deltaflight. com.br. Hang-gliding rides above Rio from Pedra Bonita mountain with instructors licensed by the **Brazilian Hang-gliding Association**.

Just Fly, T021-2268 0565, T021-9985 7540 (mob), www.justfly.com.br. Tandem flights with Paulo Celani (licensed by the **Brazilian Hang-gliding Association**) (5% discount for Footprint readers: present this book at time of reservation).

Pedro Beltrao, T021-7822 4206, pedrobeltrao77@gmail.com. One of the best and safest pilots in Brazil, with more than 20 years of experience; competitive rates. Can organize flights throughout Rio state. Highly recommended.

Ruy Marra, T021-3322 2286, www.riosuperfly.com.br, or find him at the beach. Paragliding from Leblon beach.

Hiking and climbing

Clube Excursionista Carioca, R Hilário Gouveia 71, room 206, T021-2255 1348, www.carioca.org.br. Recommended for enthusiasts, meets Wed and Fri.

Diogo Monnerat, T021-7712 7489, diogo.monnerat@gmail.com. Hiking and climbing tours in Sugar Loaf and Tijuca National Park, from beginners to experienced climbers.

Rio Hiking, T021-2552 9204 and T021-9721 0594, www.riohiking.com.br. Hiking tours around Rio city and state, including the Pedra da Gávea, Tijuca Park, Itatiaia and the Serra dos Órgãos and various city tours, including Santa Teresa.

Parachuting

Several people offer tandem jumps; check that they are accredited with the **Associação Brasileira de Vôo Livre**, www.abvl.com.br.

Barra Jumping, Aeroporto de Jacarepaguá, Av Ayrton Senna 2541, T021-3151 3602, www.barrajumping.com.br. Tandem jumping (*vôo duplo*).

Rafting

See General tours, below, for trips on the Paraibuna and Macaé rivers (both around 2 hrs from Rio).

Sea kayaking

See also **Rio Hiking**, above, for a variety of sea-kayaking tours.

Surfing

See also **Rio Surf n Stay** (page 75) and **Rio Hiking** (above) for surf lessons on Barra, Grumari and Prainha.

Nomad Surfers, www.nomadsurfers.com. Runs a surf camp in Recreio dos Bandeirantes, a stroll from Macumba beach, with simple backpacker accommodation. They offer beginners surf instruction (with attractive packages including a 7-night intensive surf school), surf board rental and surf safaris.

Other surf schools include:
Associação Brasileira de Surf Profissional, R Serzedelo Correia 15, room 804, Copacabana, T021-2235 3972, www.abrasp.com.br; **Confederação de Bodyboard do Estado do Rio de Janeiro**, R Barata Ribeiro 348/701, Copacabana, T022-2771 1802, T021-9219 3038, www.cbrasb.com.br; **Federação de Surf do Estado do Rio de Janeiro**, T021-7884 4226, www.feserj.com.br; **Organização dos Surfistas Profissionais do Rio de Janeiro**, R Visconde de Pirajá 580, shop 213, Ipanema.

Swimming

On all Rio's beaches you should take a towel or mat to protect you against sandflies. In the water stay near groups of other swimmers; there is a strong undertow.

General tours, guides and tour operators

Be A Local, T021-9643 0366, www.bealocal.com. The best of the *favela* tours with walking trips around Rocinha and money going towards community projects; trips to *baile funk* parties at weekends and to football matches.

Cultural Rio, R Santa Clara 110/904, Copacabana, T021-3322 4872 or T021-9911 3829 (mob), www.culturalrio.com.br. Tours escorted personally by Professor Carlos Roquette, English and French spoken, almost 200 options available.

Exotic Tours, T021-2179 6972, www.exotictours.com.br. Rejane Reis runs unusual trips throughout Rio, such as *candomblé*, rafting or hikes up to the Pedra da Gávea. Cultural and *favela* tours. Good English spoken.

Fábio Sombra, T021-9729 5455 (mob), fabiosombra@hotmail.com. Offers private and tailor-made guided tours focusing on the cultural aspects of Rio and Brazil.

Favela Tour, Estr das Canoas 722, bl 2, apt 125, São Conrado, T021-3322 2727, T99989 0074 (mob), www.favelatour.com.br. Safe, interesting guided tours of Rio's *favelas* in English, French, Spanish, Italian, German and Swedish (3 hrs). For the best attention and price call Marcelo Armstrong direct rather than through a hotel desk. Also offers eco-tours and river rafting.

Favela Santa Marta, T021-9177 9459, www.favelasantamartatour.blogspot.co.uk. Visits with locals to the beautifully situated Santa Marta *favela* – with stunning views of Corcovado and Sugar Loaf – and insights into local community life.

Guanatur Turismo, R Dias da Rocha 16A, Copacabana, T021-2548 3275, www.guanaturturismo.com.br. Sells long-distance bus tickets.

Helisight, R Visconde de Pirajá 580, loja 107, Térreo, Ipanema, T021-2511 2141, www.helisight.com.br. Daily from 0900. Helicopter sightseeing tours. Prices from US$90 per person for 6-7 mins from Morro de Urca or the Lagoa over Sugar Loaf and Corcovado, to US$300 per person for 30 mins over the city.

Jungle Me, T021-4105 7533, www.jungleme.com.br. Hikes in Rio off the beaten track, including the 3 peaks in Tijuca National Park (an 8-hr circuit), wild beaches and Pedra Bonita.

Metropol, R São José 46, T021-2533 5010, www.metropolturismo.com.br. Cultural, eco, and adventure tours to all parts of Brazil.

Rio Experience, T021-7567 5699, www.rioexperiencetours.com. General tours throughout Rio, including the key sights, hiking, football matches, cycle excursions and light hikes.

Rio Extreme, T021-8806 0235, www.rioextreme.com. A broad range of excursions from city tours to the key sights and nightlife excursions to hikes to the Pedra da Gávea, Itatiaia National Park and Ilha Grande.

Rio by Jeep, T021-3322 5750, T021-9693 8800, www.riobyjeep.com. 5-hr tours in open or closed jeeps with local guides showing Rio from 3 perspectives: gorgeous beaches, historical downtown and Tijuca National Park. Contact Ricardo Hamond.

Rio Turismo Radical, www.rioturismo radical.com.br. A broad menu of light adventure activities including rafting on the Rio Paraibuna, hiking, hanggliding and scuba-diving off Arraial do Cabo.

Rio Walks, T021-2516 5248, www. riowalks.com.br. Guided walks around the old city centre, the bay, the boroughs (including Santa Teresa) and the bars and botequins.

Santa Teresa Tour, T021-2507 4417, www.santateresatour.com. Historical tours around the neighbourhood run by **Rio Hiking** (see Hiking, above) in a community support project along with people from the local *favelas*.

Trilha a Pé, T021-0408 0179, www. trilhaape.com.br. Custom-made hiking trips, kayaking, surfing and light adventure tours in and around Rio.

Volleyball classes

For more general information and other schools see www.voleirio.com.br.

Escola de Vôlei Bernardinho, R das Laranjeiras 346, T021-3079 1235, www.escoladevoleibernardinho.com. br. Professional volley ball coaching for groups and individuals.

Escola de Vôlei da Leticia, Ipanema beach, between R Farme de Amoedo and R Vinicius de Moraes, T021-9841 3833, escoladevoleidaleticia@ ig.com.br, facebook: Escola-de-Volei-Letícia. Classes for adults and children in Portuguese, Mon-Fri morning and afternoon. Run by Letícia Pessoa who has been working on Ipanema since 1995.

Escola de Vôlei do Renato, Copacabana beach, in front of

R Hilário de Gouvea, T021-9544 4524, http://voleirenatofranca.blogspot. co.uk. Adults Mon-Fri 1900-2100, adult and 8-12 year olds Mon-Fri 0730-0930. Run by Renato França who has been working on the beach for 12 years.

⊖ Transport

Rio de Janeiro *p22, maps p24, p30, p33, p48, p52, p54, p60 and p62*

Air

See Getting to Rio de Janeiro, pages 6 and 23, for airport information. Metered taxis cost around US$30 from Copacabana to **Jobim International Airport**. But the pre-booked (through desks in the airport) taxi – the *taxi especial* – is safer. For the airportbased taxis you pay a fixed rate before the journey; they are very reliable but also more expensive. Other special taxis run by the meter starting at R$5.70 (US$3.31), adding R$2.46 (US$1.43) per km. There are 2 bus lines with a/c, US$5, to/from the international airport 0530-2300 and 0530-2200 from the final stop in Barra. First bus No 2018, *Via Orla da Zona Sul* (south zone shore) run from the international airport to Av Rio Branco in the centre, Flamengo, Copacabana, Ipanema, Leblon, Gavea, São Conrado, Av das Americas with a final stop at the Terminal Alvorada bus station in Barra da Tijuca and then back on the same route. Second bus No 2018, *Via Linha Amarela,* runs from the international airport to the express way Linha Amarela, Av Ayrton Senna, Aeroporto Jacarepagua, Barra

Shopping and finally Av das Americas at Barra da Tijuca and then back to the airport on the same route without a final stop. Contact **Real Auto**, T021-3035 6700, www.realautoonibus.com.br/site, for information. As well as international connections, Rio de Janeiro has flights to all the country's major airports, some via **São Paulo**, **Brasilia** or **Salvador**. The best deals on flights within Brazil are available through: **Avianca**, www.avianca.com.br; **GOL**, www.voegol.com.br; and **TAM**, www.tam.com.br.

There is a shuttle flight between **Santos Dumont Airport** and **São Paulo** (Congonhas Airport, US$250 single, US$450 return). The shuttle operates every 30 mins throughout the day 0630-2230. Sit on the right-hand side for views to São Paulo, the other side coming back; book flights in advance.

Bicycle

There are cycle paths all along Rio's beaches and the number of Carioca cyclists is on the increase. Some hostels also have bicycles for rent. Check the cycle path map on this link: www.ta.org.br/site2/index.htm. Note that the cycle path is a new space in Rio that people are learning to respect – you might find pedestrians, dogs and skaters on it. Early in the morning it's quieter. Make sure you lock the bikes well. Be careful on the roads themselves: Carioca drivers are generally disrespectful of other road users, and especially of cyclists.

Bus
Local

See also Getting around, page 26. There are good services to all parts of the city, but buses are very crowded and not for the aged or infirm during rush hours. Buses have turnstiles which are awkward if you are carrying luggage. Hang on tight as drivers live out Grand Prix fantasies. At busy times allow about 45 mins to get from Copacabana to the centre by bus. The fare on standard buses is US$1.40; suburban bus fares are up to US$3 depending on the distance. Bus stops are often not marked. The route is written on the side of the bus, but it's hard to see until the bus has actually pulled up at the stop.

Private companies, including **Real**, **Pegaso** and **Anatur**, operate a/c *frescão* buses, which can be flagged down practically anywhere. They run from all points in Rio Sul to the city centre, *rodoviária* and the airports. Fares are US$3 (US$5 to the international airport).

City Rio is an a/c tourist bus service with security guards, which runs between all the major parts of the city. Bus stops, marked by grey poles, are found where there are concentrations of hotels. Good maps show the places of interest close to each bus stop. Timetables change frequently; ask at hotels for the latest information.

Long distance

Rio's interstate bus station, the **Rodoviária Novo Rio** (see Getting there, page 26), www.novorio.com.br, is just north of the city centre and can be reached by various buses: No 326, Bancários–Castelo, from the centre and the airport; No 136: Rodoviária–Copacabana via Glória, Flamengo, and Botafogo; No127, Rodoviária–Copacabana (via Tunel do Pasmado); No 172, Rodoviária–Leblon (via Joquei and Jardim Botânico); No 128, Rodoviária–Leblon (via Copacabana and Ipanema); No 170, Rodoviária–Gávea (via Glória, Botafogo, Jardim Botânico). The area around the bus station is not safe after dark and you should beware of thieves at any time. Take a taxi to or from the nearest *metrô* station (Estácio or Praça Onze) or to your hotel. **Riotur** has a booth in the bus station that can help with hotel reservations and point you to the taxi bookings stand.

Buses run from Rio to every state capital and many smaller cities in all parts of the country from Belém in the far north to Porto Alegre and the Uruguay border in the far south. There are departures to major destinations, such as São Paulo, more than every hour. It is advisable to book in advance in high season and weekends. Travel agencies throughout the city sell tickets as do many hostels. Otherwise turn up at least 90 mins before your bus leaves to buy a ticket. Timetables, companies and platform information and the most up to date prices are available on www.novorio.com.br; type your destination into the box provided.

Most street travel agents and hostels sell *passagens de onibus* (interstate bus tickets), or will direct you to a company that does so. Agencies include **Dantur Passagens**

e Turismo, Av Rio Branco 156, subsolo loja 134, Metrô Carioca, T021-2262 3424/3624, www.dantur. com.br; **Guanatur**, R Dias da Rocha 16A, Copacabana, T021-2235 3275, www.guanaturturismo.com.br; **Paxtur Passagens**, R República do Líbano 61 loja L, Center, T021-3852 2277; and an agency at R Visconde de Pirajá 303, loja 114, Ipanema, T021-2523 1000. They charge about US$3 for bookings.

Within Rio state

To **Niteroi**, No 761D Gávea–Charitas (via Jardim Botânico and Botafogo); 751D Galeão–Charitas and 741D Leme–Charitas (via Copacabana, Botafogo, Lapa and Santos Dumont Airport), US$3. Frescões Gávea–Charitas, Galeão–Charitas; all run between Rio and Niterói.

To **Búzios**, buses leave every 2 hrs 0600-2000 daily from Rio's *rodoviária* (US$21, 2½ hrs). Go to the **1001** counter, T021-4004 5001 for tickets or buy online at www.autoviacao1001. com.br/en. Buying the ticket in advance is recommended in high season and on major holidays. You can also take any bus from Rio to the town of **Cabo Frio** (these are more frequent), from there take the Viação Salineira bus, it runs every 30 mins, US$2, from where it's 30 mins to Búzios and vice versa.

To **Petrópolis**, buses leave the *rodoviária* every 15 mins throughout the day (US$9.50) and every hour on Sun; buy tickets from **Única & Fácil** counter, www.unica-facil.com.br. The journey takes 1½ hrs. Sit on the left-hand side for the best views.

To **Angra dos Reis**, buses run at least hourly Mon-Sat from the *rodoviária* with **Costa Verde**, www.costaverdetransportes.com.br, some direct; several go through Copacabana, Ipanema and Barra then take the *via litoral*, sit on the left, US$21, 2½ hrs. You can flag down the bus in Flamengo, Copacabana, Ipanema, Barra da Tijuca, but it may well be full on Sat and bank holidays. To link up with the ferry to Ilha Grande be sure to catch a bus before 1000.

Interstate and international
Campo Grande, **Florianopolis**, **Curitiba** and **Foz do Iguaçu** are all reachable from Rio. Buses also run to **São Paulo**, **Camburiu** and **Porto Alegre**. To **Buenos Aires**, **Crucero Del Norte**, T021-2253 2960, www.crucerodelnorte.com.ar, and **Pluma**, www.pluma.com.br, run buses from the *rodoviária* via Porto Alegre and **Santa Fe** (Argentina), 48 hrs, US$146 (book 2 days in advance).

To **Santiago de Chile** (**Pluma** or **Gen Urquiza**), 70 hrs, US$197. There are no direct buses from Rio to **Asunción** (Paraguay).

Car
Service stations are closed in many places on Sat and Sun. Road signs are notoriously misleading in Rio and you can end up in a *favela* (take special care if driving along the Estr da Gávea to São Conrado as it is possible to unwittingly enter Rocinha, Rio's biggest slum).

Car hire
There are many agencies on Av Princesa Isabel, Copacabana. A credit card is essential for hiring a car. Recent reports suggest it is cheaper to hire outside Brazil; you may also obtain more comprehensive insurance this way. **Avis**, Antônio Carlos Jobim International Airport, T021-3398 5060, Santos Dumont Airport, T021-3814 7378, Av Princesa Isabel 150A and B, Copacabana, T021-2543 8481, www.avis.com.br; **Hertz**, international airport, T021-3398 4338, Av Princesa Isabel 500, Copacabana, T021-2275 7440; **Localiza**, international airport, T021-3398 3107, and Santos Dumont Airport, T0800-992000, Av Princesa Isabel 150, Copacabana, T021-2275 3340; **Nobre**, Av Princesa Isabel 7, Copacabana, T021-2295 1799; **Telecar**, R Figueiredo Magalhães 701, Copacabana, T021-2548 6778.

Ferry
Every 10 mins ferries and launches cross Guanabara Bay for **Niterói** from the 'Barcas' terminal at Praça 15 de Novembro, www.barcas-sa.com.br. The journey takes 20-30 mins and costs US$1.70. Catamarans (*aerobarcas*) also leave every 10 mins but take just 12 mins and cost US$1.70 (same price as a *barca* ferry). There are also more expensive catamarans and motor boats that take 9 mins. The slow, cheaper ferry gives the best views. From Niterói, ferries and catamarans return to Rio de Janeiro from the city centre terminal at Praça Araribóia and at Charitas district.

Metrô

See page 26 and map, below, www.metrorio.com.br. The current 2 metrô lines are fast, clean, a/c and safe. Most stations are open Mon-Fri 0500-2400 (though a few close as early as 1700; check website for timetable); Sat 0500-2400 (with some stations closing at 1400); Sun and bank holiday 0700-2300 (with at least 25% of stations not opening at all). During Carnaval most stations are open 24 hrs. A single fare costs R$3.50 (US$1.75). Multi-tickets and integrated bus/metrô tickets are available with connections as far as Barra and Jacarepaguá (on express buses). There is also a pre-paid card, **Cartão Pré-Pago**; the minimal initial payment is US$5, any minimal additional after that US$2.50. These can only be bought at the stations. Free metrô maps are available at the counter. Note that Rio metrô has a women-only designated wagon Mon-Fri 0600-0900 and 1700-2000; it is the last wagon of each train, and has

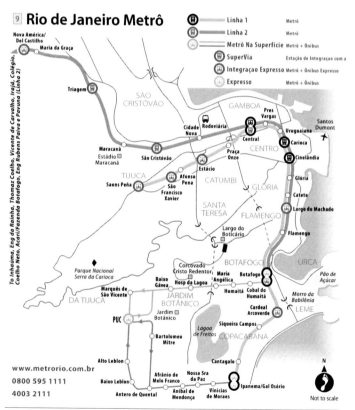

9 Rio de Janeiro Metrô

a pink stripe across the top, but many women still prefer to travel with men, and often some distracted men pop into the pink wagon.

Substantial changes in bus operations are taking place because of the extended *metrô* system; buses connecting with the *metrô* have a blue-and-white symbol in the windscreen. **Line 1 (Orange)** operates between the inner suburb of Tijuca (station Saens Peña), to Ipanema (station General Osório) via the railway station (Central), Glória, Botafogo and Arcoverde. **Line 2 (Green)** runs from the northern outskirt suburb of Pavuna to Botafogo, passing Engenho da Rainha, the Maracanã stadium, Central and then goes along the shore parallel to Line 1.

By 2016 Rio has committed itself to building a new line (**Linha 4**) between the city centre and Barra da Tijuca in the south, in time for the Olympics in 2016. However, it has taken 8 years to complete the last 2 *metrô* stations in Copacabana and Ipanema so some are sceptical. There are also even grander plans to build **Linha 3** to Niterói via an underwater tunnel beneath Guanabara Bay, however this is not scheduled for completion before the 2016 Olympics.

Taxi

See also Getting around, page 27. The common taxis in Rio are yellow and blue, and use meters. There are 2 price bands, and there is a little flag on the meter that the driver tugs to choose the band. Bandeira 1 runs Mon-Sat 0600-2100, with the meter starting at R$4.30 (US$2.50) and then adding R$1.40 (US$0.81) per km.

Bandeira 2 runs Mon-Sat 2100-0600, Sun and bank holidays, it starts at R$5.70 (US$3.32) adding R$2.46 (US$1.43) per km. The websites www.taxisimples.com.br/rio-de-janeiro, www.tarifadetaxi.com/rio-de-janeiro have a Rio map and calculate the approximate taxi price for you. The fare between Copacabana and the centre is around US$30. It's a good idea to print out a copy of the map and keep it handy so you can monitor your journey; some taxis drivers sneakily choose the long way round in order to overcharge. Also, make sure meters are cleared and on the right price band. Taxis have red number plates with white digits (yellow for private cars, with black digits). Smaller ones (mostly Volkswagen) are marked 'TAXI' on the windscreen or roof. It is safest to use taxis from *pontos* (taxi ranks), which are abundant throughout the city. *Ponto* taxis have the name of the *ponto* painted on the outside, indicating which *ponto* they belong to. Radio taxis are safer but almost twice as expensive; each co-op has a different colour: **Central Táxi**, yellow and blue, T021-2195 1000, www.centraltaxi.com.br; **Coopacarioca**, yellow and blue, T021-2158 1818, www.cooparioca.com.br; **Coopertramo**, white, T021-2209 9292, www.radio-taxi.com.br; **Cootramo**, blue, T021-3976 9944, www.cootramo.com.br; **Transcoopass**, red, T021-2209 1555, www.transcoopass.com.br. If you get a radio/co-op taxi (taxi especial) at the airport you pay in advance, buying the ticket at a special booth. In this case the meter will be off; but if you get into one outside the airport, the meter should be turned on. It will cost you US$40-45 to Copacabana or Ipanema. It is better to buy the ticket in advance – you will know for sure how much you are paying.

Train
Buses marked 'E Ferro' go to the train station. There are suburban trains to **Nova Iguaçu**, **Nilópolis**, **Campo Grande** and elsewhere. **Supervia** is the main company that sells tickets, www.supervia.com.br. None of the destinations are of tourist interest and they can be rough and dangerous, mainly at night. The station **Central do Brasil** is worth a visit and occasionally hosts cultural events and music concerts; check the program on the Supervia website.

Tram
See also Getting around, page 27, and Santa Teresa, page 47. The last remaining tram runs from near the Largo da Carioca (there is a museum open Fri 0830-1700) across the old aqueduct (Arcos) to Dois Irmãos or Paula Mattos in **Santa Teresa**; a historical and interesting journey, US$0.40.

⊙ Directory

Rio de Janeiro *p22, maps p24, p30, p33, p48, p52, p54, p60 and p62*

Banks
Branches of **Bradesco, Banco 24 Horas** and **Banco do Brasil**
throughout the city. ATMs do not function late at night after 2200.

Embassies and consulates
Argentina, Praia de Botafogo 228/201, T021-2553 1646, Mon-Fri, 1000-1300 and 1330-1530, very helpful for visas; **Australia**, Av Presidente Wilson 231 23rd floor, T021-3824 4624, honconau@terra.com.br; **Austria**, Av Atlântica 3804, Copacabana, T021-2102 0020; **Canada**, Av Atlântica 1130, 5th floor, Copacabana, T021-2543 3004; **Denmark**, Av Rio Branco 45, sala 1902, T021-3466 6466; **France**, Av Pres Antônio Carlos 58, T021-3974 6699; **Germany**, R Pres Carlos de Campos 417, T021-2554 0004; **Israel**, Av NS de Copacabana 680, T021-2548 5432; **Netherlands**, Praia de Botafogo 242, 10th floor, T021-2552 9028 (Dutch newspapers here and at KLM office on Av Rio Branco); **Paraguay**, same address, 2nd floor, T021-2553 2294, visas US$5; **Sweden**, **Finland** and **Norway**, Praia do Flamengo 344, 9th floor, T021-2553 5505; **Switzerland**, R Cândido Mendes 157, 11th floor, T021-2221 1867; **UK**, Praia do Flamengo 284, 2nd floor, T021-2555 9600, T021-2553 3223 (consular section direct line), consular section is open Mon-Fri 0900-1230 (consulate 0830-1700), Metrô Flamengo, or bus No 170, the consulate issues a useful *Guidance for Tourists* pamphlet; **Uruguay**, Praia de Botafogo 242, 6th floor, T021-2553 6030; **USA**, Av Pres Wilson 147, T021-2292 7117, Mon-Fri 0800-1100, passports 1330-1500.

Immigration

Federal Police, Av Rodrigues Alves, 13th floor, Centro, T021-2203 4000. To renew a 90-day visa, US$45. Renew at least a week before your visa runs out and allow 4 hrs for the bureaucratic process of queuing and form filling.

Internet

Internet cafés are easy to find. There are several places in **Rio Sul** shopping centre, Botafogo; many on Av NS de Copacabana, and others on R Visconde de Pirajá, Ipanema. **Phone Serv**, Av NS de Copacabana 454, loja B, US$3 per hr internet, telephone service. **Tudo é Fácil** has 3 branches in Copacabana: R Xavier da Silveira 19; Av Prado Júnior 78; and R Barata Ribeiro 396, www.tudoefacil.com.br. Well organized, with identification cards so once registered you can bypass the front desk, telephone booths and scanners, US$2 per hr, discounts for extended use.

Language courses

Instituto Brasil-Estados Unidos, Av N Sra de Copacabana 690, 5th floor, www.ibeu.org.br, 8-week course, 3 classes a week, US$150, 5-week intensive course US$260, good English library at same address; **IGI Instituto Globus de Idiomas**, R do Catete 310, sala 303/305, www.institutoglobus.com.br, US$26 per hr for individual lessons, cheaper for groups, helpful staff, recommended.

Medical services

Hospital Miguel Couto, Mário Ribeiro 117, Gávea, T021-3111 3800, free casualty ward. **Hospital Municipal Rocha Maia**, R Gen Severiano 91, Botafogo, T021-2295 2295/2121, near Rio Sul shopping centre, a good public hospital for minor injuries and ailments; free, but may be queues; **Policlínica**, Av Nilo Peçanha 38, www.pgrj.org.br, for diagnosis and investigation. **Saúde dos Portos**, Praça Mcal Âncora, T021-2240 8628/ 8678, Mon-Fri 1000-1100, 1500-1800, for vaccinations; vaccination book and ID required.

Post

The **Central Post Office** is on R 1 de Março 64, at the corner of R do Rosário, www.correios.com.br. Also at Av NS de Copacabana 540 and many other locations. All handle international post. There is a post office at Antônio Carlos Jobim International Airport. **Federal Express**, R Nair 135, Olaria, is reliable. **Poste Restante** at **Correios**, Av NS de Copacabana 540 and all large post offices (letters held for a month, recommended, US$0.10 per letter).

Students

Student Travel Bureau, Av Nilo Peçanha 50, SL 2417, Centro, T021-2544 2627; and R Visconde de Pirajá 550, loja 201, Ipanema, T021-25 12 8577, www.stb.com.br, has details of travel, discounts and cultural exchanges for ISIC holders.

Toilets

There are very few public toilets in Rio de Janeiro, but shopping centres, many bars and restaurants (eg McDonald's) offer facilities. Just ask for the *banheiro*.

East of Rio de Janeiro

Rio de Janeiro state is one of Brazil's smallest, but it is packed with great things to see. East of Rio the country gets drier and looks more Mediterranean. The coast, which is lined with fabulous beaches for hundreds of kilometres, is backed by a long series of saltwater lakes and drifting sand dunes. Most visitors ignore Niterói, the city immediately opposite Rio across Guanabara Bay, despite the fact is ocean beaches as good as or better than Rio's. Instead, they head straight for the surf towns around Cabo Frio or the fashionable little resort of Búzios, which has good beaches and lively summer nightlife.

Niterói → *For listings, see pages 110-115.*

Cariocas are rude about everywhere, but they are especially rude about their neighbour across Guanabara Bay. The only good thing about Niterói, they say, is the view it has of Rio de Janeiro. As a result few visitors make it here. However, its ocean beaches are less polluted and far less crowded than Rio's and the views from them across the bay, especially at sunset, are wonderful. Oscar Niemeyer's Museu de Arte Contemporânea, a flying-saucer-shaped building perched on a promontory, is one of his very best buildings. There is no reason to stay overnight in Niterói but the city is well worth visiting as a day trip or on the way to Búzios.

Arriving in Niterói
Getting there Ferries and launches to Niterói leave from the 'Barcas' terminal at Praça 15 de Novembro in central Rio, www.barcas-sa.com.br. Boats run every 10 minutes and the journey takes 20-30 minutes, US$1.70. *Aerobarcas* (catamarans) take just three minutes and cost US$1.70. Boats arrive at the Praça Araribóia city centre terminal in Niterói and at Charitas district.

Bus Nos 761D Gávea–Charitas (via Jardim Botânico and Botafogo), 751D Galeão–Charitas, and 741D Leme-Charitas (via Copacabana, Botafogo, Lapa and Santos Dumont Airport), US$3, and Frescões Gávea–Charitas, Galeão–Charitas, all run between Rio and Niterói. If you are driving, the bridge across Guanabara Bay is well signposted; there is a toll of US$2.50 per car.

Getting around To get to the ocean beaches from Niterói, take bus Nos 38 or 52 from Praça General Gomes Carneiro or a bus from the street directly ahead of the ferry entrance, at right angles to the coast road. For Jurujuba take bus No 33 from the boat dock; sit on the right-hand side, it's a beautiful ride.

Tourist information Contact Neltur ⓘ *Estrada Leopoldo Fróes 773, São Francisco, T021-2710 2727, www.niteroiturismo.com.br.*

Places in Niterói

Surrounded by long curved walkways, the space-age building of the **Museu de Arte Contemporânea** ⓘ *Mirante da Boa Viagem, T021-2620 2400, www. macniteroi.com.br, Tue-Sun 1100-1800, US$2.90, free Wed,* is rapidly becoming the most famous work by Brazil's celebrated disciple of Le Corbusier, Oscar Niemeyer. It is in a fabulous location, sitting above a long beach with a sweeping view across Guanabara Bay to Rio as a backdrop. The building itself looks like a Gerry Anderson vision of the future; one can almost imagine *Thunderbird 1* taking off through its centre. The main gallery is a white circle of polished concrete perched on a low monopod and sitting in a reflection pool. It is reached by a coiling, serpentine ramp which meets the building on its second storey. The exhibitions comprise seasonal shows and a permanent collection of Brazilian contemporary art of all disciplines. The top level is devoted to temporary displays and the intermediate to the permanent collection. Niemeyer overcomes the problem of the unsuitability of a curved space for the exhibition of art by using an inner hexagonal core enclosed by flat screen walls. More difficult to overcome is that the glimpses of the stunning panorama of Rio through the gaps in the hexagon are far more captivating than most of the art. The building is worth seeing at dusk when it is lit; the sky above the streetlights of Rio is light peacock blue infused with lilac and the distant figure of the Corcovado Christ shines brilliant xenon-white over the dark mass of mountains.

Many buildings associated with the city's period as state capital are grouped around the **Praça da República**. None are open to the public. The city's main thoroughfare, Avenida Ernâni do Amaral Peixoto, runs from the *praça* and is lined with buildings similar to Avenida Presidente Vargas in Rio. At the end of the avenue is the dock for Rio, a statue of the indigenous chief, Araribóia, and the **Bay Market Shopping Centre**.

Perched on a rocky promontory at the mouth of Guanabara Bay, the 16th-century **Fortaleza Santa Cruz** ⓘ *Estrada General Eurico Gaspar Dutra, Jurujuba, T021-2711 0462, Tue-Sun 0900-1600, US$2, compulsory guided tour in Portuguese only,* is still used by the Brazilian military and is the most important historical monument in Niterói. As well as the usual range of cannon, dungeons and bulwarks the tour includes a visit to gruesome execution sites and a little chapel dedicated to Saint Barbara. The statue of the saint inside was originally destined for Santa Cruz dos Militares in Rio. However, unlike most Cariocas, the saint obviously prefers Niterói: any attempts to move her image from here have allegedly been accompanied by violent storms.

Beaches

The beaches closest to the city centre are unsuitable for bathing (Gragoatá, Vermelha, Boa Viagem, das Flechas). The next beaches along, also in the city and with polluted water, have more in the way of restaurants, bars and nightlife and some of the best views in the whole country, especially at sunset and sunrise. Icaraí is the smartest district, with the best hotels and good nightlife. There are superb views of Rio from here, especially at sunset, Neighbouring **São Francisco** and **Charitas** also have good views. The road continues round the bay, past Preventório and Samanguaiá to **Jurujuba**, a fishing village at the end of the No 33 bus route. About 2 km from Jurujuba along a narrow road are the attractive twin beaches of **Adão** and **Eva** beneath the Fortaleza Santa Cruz with more lovely views of Rio across the bay. These beaches are often used for *candomblé* (Brazilian-African spirit religion) ceremonies.

About 40 minutes from Niterói, through picturesque countryside, are four fabulous stretches of sand, the best in the area: **Piratininga**, **Camboinhas**, **Itaipu** and **Itacoatiara**. Buses leave from the street directly ahead of the ferry entrance, at right angles to the coast road. The undertow at Itacoatiara is dangerous, but the waves are popular with surfers and the beach itself is safe. Itaipu is also used by surfers.

Costa do Sol → *For listings, see pages 110-115.*

To the east of Niterói lies a series of saltwater lagoons, the **Lagos Fluminenses**. Two small lakes lie behind the beaches of Piratininga, Itaipu and Itacoatiara, but they are polluted and ringed by mud. The next lakes, **Maricá** and **Saquarema**, are much larger; although they are still muddy, the waters are relatively unpolluted and wildlife abounds in the scrub and bush around the lagoons. This is a prime example of the *restinga* (coastal swamp and forest) environment. The RJ-106 road runs behind the lakes en route to Cabo Frio and Búzios, but an unmade road goes along the coast between Itacoatiara and Cabo Frio, giving access to the many long, open beaches of Brazil's Costa do Sol. The whole area is perfect for camping.

Saquarema → *Phone code: 022. Population: 44,000.*

Saquarema is a fishing and holiday village, known as the centre for surfing in Brazil. Its cold, open seas provide consistent crashing waves of up to 3 m.

Frequent national and international championships take place here, but beware of strong currents. The lovely white church of **Nossa Senhora de Nazaré** (1675) is on a green promontory jutting into the ocean. Local legend has it that on 8 September 1630, fishermen, saved from a terrible storm, found an image of the Virgem de Nazaré in the rocks. A chapel was founded on the spot and subsequent attempts to relocate the Virgin (as when the chapel was falling into disrepair) resulted in her miraculously returning to the original site. For **tourist information** ① *R Coronel Madureira 77, Centro Saquarema, T022-9972 7251, www.saquarema.rj.gov.br.*

Araruama → *Phone code: 022. Population: 66,500.*

The **Lagoa Araruama** (220 sq km) is one of the largest lakes in Brazil and is famous for its medicinal mud. The salinity is high, the waters calm and almost the entire lake is surrounded by sandy beaches, making it popular with families looking for unpolluted bathing. The constant breeze makes the lake perfect for windsurfing and sailing.

At the eastern end of the lake, also inland, is **São Pedro de Aldeia**, which has a population of 55,500 and, despite intensive development, still retains much of its colonial charm. There is a lovely **Jesuit church** built in 1723, and a **tourist office** ① *Av Brasil 655, Parque Hotel, T022-2665 4145, www.araruama.rj.gov.br.*

Arraial do Cabo → *Phone code: 022. Population: 21,500.*

This rather ugly little salt-industry town near Cabo Frio is considerably less busy than the resort at Cabo Frio a little to the north, and provides access to equally good beaches and dunes. The lake and the ocean here are divided by the Restinga de Massambaba, a long spit of sand mostly deserted except for the beaches of **Massambaba** and **Seca**, at the western end, and **Grande** in the east at Arraial do Cabo town itself. Arraial has lots of other small beaches on the bays and islands that form the cape, round which the line of the coast turns north, including the long, busy stretch at **Anjos**, **Praia do Forno** and **Prainha**. Excursions can be made by boat around the islets and by jeep or buggy over the sand dunes.

Arriving in Arraial do Cabo A very steep road connects the beaches of Itaipu and Itacoatiara with RJ-106 (and on to Bacaxá and Araruama) via the village of Itaipu-Açu. Most maps do not show a road beyond Itaipu-Açu; it is certainly too steep for buses. An alternative to the route from Niterói to Araruama through the lagoons is further inland than the RJ-106, via Manilha, Itaboraí and Rio Bonito on the BR-101 and RJ-124; this is a fruit-growing region.

Diving and adventure sports While Arraial is not a dive destination of international quality in its own right, it is one of the best in Brazil and there are a number of sites of varying difficulty with caverns and swim-throughs that are well worth exploring. Cold and warm currents meet here just off the coast and the marine life is more abundant than almost anywhere else on mainland southern Brazil. Expect to see schools of tropical and subtropical reef fish such as batfish and various tangs and butterfly fish, the occasional turtle, colonies of gorgonians and beautiful (though invasive) soft corals probably brought here on oil tankers from the Indo-Pacific. Dolphins are frequent visitors. The best visibility is between November and May. Water temperature is always below 20°C. The little town is also establishing itself as an adventure sports destination with activities including dune boarding, parachuting, kitesurfing and kayaking available. ▸▸ *See What to do, page 113.*

Excursions Praia do Farol, on Ilha do Cabo Frio, is one of Brazil's best beaches, with sand dunes and crystal-clear water. The **tourist office** ① *T022-2622 1949, www.arraialdocabo-rj.com.br/zarony.html,* is at Praça da Bandeira. ▸▸ *See What to do, page 114.*

Cabo Frio → *For listings, see pages 110-115. Phone code: 022. Population: 127,000.*

This busy tourist town, 168 km from Rio, is a popular middle-class Brazilian seaside resort, which overflows at the weekend with Cariocas. Although the town itself is very touristy, there are some attractive white-sand beaches, some with dunes and good surf and windsurfing, and accommodation nearby. Bring mosquito repellent.

Cabo Frio vies with Porto Seguro for the title of Brazil's first city. The navigator Amerigo Vespucci landed here in 1503 and returned to Portugal with a boatload of *pau brasil*. Since the wood in these parts was of better quality than that further north, the area subsequently became the target for loggers from France, the Netherlands and England. The Portuguese failed to capitalize on their colony here and it was the French who established the first defended settlement. Eventually the Portuguese took it by force but it was not until the second decade of the 17th century that they planned their own fortification, the **Forte São Mateus** ① *daily 0800-1800,* which was started in 1618 on the foundations of the French fort. It is now a ruin at the mouth of the Canal de Itajuru, with rusting cannons propped up against its whitewashed ramparts. The canal connects Lagoa Araruama with the ocean.

The town beach, **Praia do Forte**, is highly developed and stretches south for about 7.5 km to Arraial do Cabo, its name changing to **Praia das Dunas** (after the dunes) and **Praia do Foguete**. These waters are much more suited to surfing. North of the canal entrance and town is the small under-developed beach of **Praia Brava** (popular with surfers and naturists) and the wine-glass bay of **Praia das Conchas**, which has a few shack restaurants. Next is **Praia do Peró**, 7 km of surf and sand on the open sea with a small town behind it and cheap accommodation. The best dunes are at Peró, Dama Branca (on road to Arraial) and the Pontal dunes at Praia do Forte.

Arriving in Cabo Frio The **airport** ⓘ *Estrada Velha do Arraial do Cabo s/n, T022-2647 9500, www.aeroportocabofrio.com.br*, receives flights in high season only, from Rio, Belo Horizonte and São Paulo, Ribeirão Preto and Uberlândia. The **tourist office** ⓘ *Av do Contorno s/n, Algodoal, T022-2647 1689, www.cabofrio. tur.br or www.cabofrioturismo.rj.gov.br*, is in the big orange building.

Búzios → *For listings, see pages 110-115. Phone code: 022. Population: 18,000.*

Búzios is the principal resort of choice for Carioca and Mineira upper-middle classes searching for their idea of St Tropez sophistication. When it was discovered by Brigitte Bardot in 1964 it was little more than a collection of colonial fishermen's huts and a series of pristine beaches hidden beneath steep hills covered in maquis-like vegetation. Now there are strings of hotels behind all of those beaches and the huts have become lost within a designated tourist village of bars, bikini boutiques and restaurants, most of which are strung along the pretty little main street, **Rua das Pedras**. Bardot sits here too – cheesily immortalized in brass, and subsequently in tens of thousands of pictures taken by the troops of cruise line passengers who fill the streets of Búzios in high season. St Tropez this is not, but it can be fun for 20-somethings who are single and looking not to stay that way. The beaches are beautiful and there are a few romantic hotels with wonderful views.

Arriving in Búzios
Getting there Buses leave almost every hour 0600-2000 daily from Rio's *rodoviária* (US$21, 2½ hours). Tickets can be bought from the **1001** counter, T022-4004 5001, or buy online at www.autoviacao1001.com.br/en. Buying the ticket in advance is recommended in high season and on major holidays. You can also take any bus from Rio to the town of Cabo Frio (buses are more frequent); from Cabo Frio take the Viação Salineira bus, US$5 – it's 30 minutes to Búzios. The Búzios *rodoviária* is a few blocks' walk from the centre. Some *pousadas* are within 10 minutes' walk, while for others you'll need to take a local bus (R$2.70/US$1.35) or taxi. The buses from Cabo Frio run the length of the peninsula and pass several *pousadas*. The journey by car along the BR-106 takes about 2½ hours from Rio. Traffic back to Rio can be appalling on Sunday nights and during the peak holiday season.

Tourist information The main **tourist office** ① *Manguinhos, Pórtico de Búzios s/n, T022-2633 6200, T0800-249999, www.buziosturismo.com, 24 hrs,* is at the entrance to town on the western edge of the peninsula. It has helpful staff, some of whom speak English. There's another office at Praça Santos Dumont (T022-2623 2099), in the centre of Búzios, which is more limited. For most of the hotels and services on the peninsula check www.buziosonline.com.br or www.buzios.rj.gov.br. Maps are available from hotels and tourist offices.

Beaches

During the daytime, the best option is to head for the beaches, of which there are 25. The most visited are **Geribá** (many bars and restaurants; popular with surfers), **Ferradura** (deep-blue sea and calm waters), **Ossos** (the most famous and close to the centre), **Tartaruga** and **João Fernandes**. The better surf beaches, such as **Praia de Manguinhos** and **Praia de Tucuns**, are further from the town centre. To help you to decide which beach suits you best, you can join one of the local two- or three-hour schooner trips (contact **Buziana** ① *T022-2623 2922, www.buzianatour.com.br, US$30,* which pass many of the beaches, or hire a beach buggy (available from agencies on Rua das Pedras or through most hotels and hostels).

East of Rio de Janeiro listings

For hotel and restaurant price codes and other relevant information, see pages 9-13.

⊜ Where to stay

Niterói *p104*
$$$ Icaraí Praia, R Belizário Augusto 21, T021-2612 5030, www. icaraipraiahotel.com.br. Plain rooms in a faded 1980s beachfront tower.
$$$ Tower Hotel, Av Almte Ari Parreiras 12, Icaraí, T021-2612 2121, www.towerhotel.com.br. Niterói's smartest hotel (3-star) with ordinary, rather faded rooms, an indoor pool, sauna and reasonable business facilities.

Saquarema *p106*
$$ Pousada do Holandês, Av Vilamar 377, Itaúna beach, www.pousada doholandes.com.br. Many languages spoken by Dutch owner and his Brazilian wife. Good meals – follow the signs, or take a taxi, from Saquarema. Recommended.
$$ Pousada Pedra d'Água Maasai, Trav de Itaúna 17, Praia de Itaúna, T022-2651 1092, www.maasai.com.br. Good little beachfront hotel with 18 apartments, pool, sauna and a reasonable seafood restaurant.

Araruama *p107*
$$$ Enseada das Garças, R José Costa 1088, Ponta da Areia, about 5 km from São Pedro de Aldeia,

T022-2621 1924, www.enseadadas garcas.com.br. Beautiful little hotel overlooking the sea with access to good walking trails.

Arraial do Cabo *p107*
$$$ Pousada Nautillu's, R Marcílio Dias 100, T022-2622 1611, www. pousadanautillus.com.br. Medium-sized *pousada* with a pool, sauna, bar and restaurant. Recommended.

Cabo Frio *p108*
$$$ La Plage, R das Badejos 40, Peró, T022-2647 1746, www.laplage.com.br. Cheaper in low season. Fully equipped suites; those upstairs have a sea view, excellent for families. Right on the beach, services include pool and bar, à la carte restaurant, hydro-massage, sauna, 24-hr cyber café, garage.
$$ Pousada São Lucas, R Goiás 266, Jardim Excelsior, T022-2645 3037, www.pousadasaolucas.com.br (formerly a youth hostel). 3 mins from the *rodoviária*. Price is for double room with TV. Also has dorms with hot shower, breakfast and fan (a little cheaper in low season).

Búzios *p109*
Rooms in Búzios are overpriced and during peak season, over-booked. Prior reservations are needed in summer, during holidays such as Carnaval and New Year's Eve, and at weekends. For cheaper options and better availability, try Cabo Frio.

Several private houses rent rooms, especially in summer and holidays. Look for the signs: *'Alugo quartos'*.
$$$$ Casas Brancas, Alto do Humaitá 10, T022-2623 1458, www. casasbrancas.com.br. Mock-Mykonos buildings with separate terraces for the pool and spa areas. Sweeping views over the bay. Wonderfully romantic at night when it is lit by candlelight. If you can't afford to stay, come for dinner. The **Abracadabra** (www.abracadabrapousada.com.br) next door is owned by **Casas Brancas** and is similar though cheaper and less stylish.
$$$$ Pousada Byblos, Alto do Humaitá 14, T022-2623 1162, www. byblos.com.br. Wonderful views out over the bay and bright, light rooms with tiled floors and balconies.

$$$ Pousada Santorini, R 9, Lote 28, Quadra C, Praia João Fernandes, T022-2623 2802, www.pousadasantorini. com.br. Good service, lovely beach views from a maquis-covered ridge, clean mock-Greek island design and spacious rooms and public areas.

$$$ Pousada Hibiscus Beach, R 1 No 22, quadra C, Praia de João Fernandes, T022-2623 6221, www. hibiscusbeach.com. A peaceful spot, run by its British owners, overlooking Praia de João Fernandes, 15 pleasant bungalows, a/c, satellite TV, garden, pool, light meals available, help with car/buggy rentals and local excursions. One of the best beach hotels.

$$$ Pousada Pedra da Laguna, R 6, lote 6, Praia da Ferradura, T022-2623 1965, www.pedradalaguna. com.br. Spacious rooms, the best with a view, 150 m from the beach. Part of the **Roteiros de Charme** group.

$$ Praia dos Amores, Av José Bento Ribeiro Dantas 92, T022-2623 2422, www.alberguedebuzios.com.br. IYHA, not far from the bus station, next to Praia da Tartaruga and just under 1 km from the centre. About the best value in Búzios.

$$ Ville Blanche, R Manoel T de Farias, 222, T022-2623 1201, http:// villeblanchebuzios.blogspot.co.uk. A hostel and hotel right in the centre in the street parallel to R da Pedras with a/c dorms for up to 10, and light-blue tiled doubles with fridges, en suites and a balcony. Can be noisy.

🍴 Restaurants

Niterói p104
$$$ Olimpo, Estação Hidroviária de Charitas, 2nd floor, Av Quintino Bocaiúva, s/n, Charitas, T021-2711 0554, www.restauranteolimpo.com.br. Brazilian and European cooking in a Niemyer building surrounded by windows overlooking Guanabara Bay.

$$ La Sagrada Familia, R Domingues de Sá 325, Icaraí, T021-2610 1683, www.lasagrada familia.com.br/niteroi. htm. The best restaurant in Niterói, housed in a beautiful colonial building, with a varied menu and reasonable wine list.

Cabo Frio p108
The neat row of restaurants on Av dos Pescadores are worth a browse for good-value seafood and pasta. They have French-style seating on the pavement under awnings.

$$$-$$ Picolino, R Mcal F Peixoto 319, Blvd Canal, T022-2647 6222, www.restaurantepicolino.com.br. In a nice old building, very smart, with a mixed menu of seafood and a few international dishes.

Búzios p109
See also **Casas Brancas**, page 111 (fine views and romantic dining).

$$$ Satyricon, Av José Bento Ribeiro Dantas 500, Orla Bardot Praia da Armação (in front of Morro da Humaitá), T022-2623 2691. The most illustrious restaurant in Búzios, specializing in Italian seafood. Decent wine list.

$$$ Sawasdee Bistrô, Av José Bento Ribeiro Dantas 422, Orla Bardot, T022-2623 4644. Marcos Sodré's Brazilian take on Thai (and Indonesian) food is strong on flavour but very light on spice (for those used to genuine article). Try the tom yam prawn and coconut milk soup made with crustaceans brought in straight from the sea. Vegetarian options.
$$$-$$ O Barco, Av José Bento Ribeiro Dantas 1054, Orla Bardot, T022-2629 8307. Very simple restaurant overlooking the water, run and owned by a fishmonger, and offering the freshest seafood. Come early to ensure a table. Very popular.

🎧 Bars and clubs

Búzios *p109*
In season, nightlife in Búzios is young, beautiful and buzzing. Out of season it is non-existent. Most of the bars and the handful of clubs are on Orla Bardot. These include **Zapata**, a bizarrely shaped Mexican theme-bar and restaurant with dancing and electronica; and **Privilege**, Av José Bento Ribeiro Dantas 550 (Orla Bardot). **Pacha**, R das Pedras 151, T021-2292 9606, www.pachabuzios. com, is Búzios's main club and the sister of its namesake in Ibiza, with pumping techno, house and hip-hop and cavernous dance floor. There are plenty of others on and around Av José Bento Ribeiro Dantas.

⚙ Festivals

Niterói *p104*
Mar-May Festa do Divino, a festival that traditionally begins on Easter Sun and continues for the next 40 days, in which the *bandeira* (banner) *do Divino* is taken around the local municipalities. The festival ends at Pentecost with sacred and secular celebrations.

🛍 Shopping

Búzios *p109*
Many of Brazil's fashionable and beautiful come here for their holidays and Búzios is therefore a good place to pick up the kind of beach clothes and tropical cuts that they would wear. Although seemingly expensive these clothes are a fraction of what you would pay for labels of this quality in Europe, the US or Australia. Shopping is best on R das Pedras. Aside from the boutiques, there is little else of interest beyond the expected range of tourist tack shops. Of the boutiques the best are as follows:

⚙ What to do

Arraial do Cabo *p107*
Deep Trip, Av Getulio Vargas 93, Praia Grande, Arraial do Cabo, T021-9942 3020 (mob), www.deeptrip.com.br. The only PADI-affiliated dive operator in Arraial, with a range of courses and dive trips.
Gas, Av Litoranea 80, Praia Grande, T022-9956 1222, www.arraialdocabo-rj.com.br/gas. Various adventure

sports including dune boarding, parachuting and kayak surfing. Runs dive trips but is not PADI accredited. **K-Kite School**, R da Alegria 15, T021-9351 7164, www.kkite.hpg. ig.com.br. Windsurfing and kitesurfing, and lessons.

Trips to Ilha do Cabo Frio
Barco Lindo Olhar, T022-2647 4493, ask for Vadinho or Eraldo in the town's main marina.
Zarony Tours, Marina dos Pescadores, 2nd pier on Praia dos Anjos, T022-7836 7952 (mob), www.arraialdocabo-rj.com.br/zarony.html.

Búzios *p109*
Malizia, Av José Bento Ribeiro Dantas, Orla Bardot, T022-2623 2022, www. maliziatour.com.br. Money exchange, car hire and other services.
Mister Tours, R Germiniano J Luís 3, Centro, T022-2623 2100, www.mistertours.com.br.

⊖ Transport

Niterói *p104*
Boat Ferries and launches run between the terminal at Praça Araribóia (for Niteroi city centre) and Charitas beach and the 'Barcas' terminal at Praça 15 de Novembro in **Rio de Janeiro** city centre, every 10 mins (20-30 mins, US$1.70), www.barcas-sa.com.br. There are also catamarans (*aerobarcas*) every 10 mins (12 mins, US$1.70). The slow, cheaper ferry gives the best views.

Bus Buses running between Niterói and **Rio de Janeiro** include No 761D Gávea–Charitas (via Jardim Botânico and Botafogo), 751D Aeroporto Galeão–Charitas 740-D and 741D Leme–Charitas (via Copacabana, Botafogo, Lapa and Santos Dumont Airport), US$3. Also available are Frescões Gávea–Charitas, Galeão–Charitas.

Saquarema *p106*
Bus To **Rio de Janeiro (Mil e Um, 1001)**, www.autoviacao1001.com. br/en, every 2 hrs 0625-1950, about 2 hrs, US$10.

Arraial do Cabo *p107*
Bus To **Rio de Janeiro**, www. autoviacao1001.com.br/en, US$17.

Cabo Frio *p108*
Air Flights in high season to **Rio de Janeiro**, **Belo Horizonte**, **Sao Paulo**, **Ribeirão Preto**, and **Uberlândia** with GOL, www.voegol.com.br.

Local bus **Salineira** and **Montes Brancos** run the local services. US$1.35 to places such as **Búzios**, **São Pedro da Aldeia**, **Saquarema**, **Araruama**, **Arraial do Cabo**. The urban bus terminal is near Largo de Santo Antônio, opposite the BR petrol station. **Long distance bus** The inter-city and interstate *rodoviária* is 2 km from the centre. Buses to **Rio de Janeiro** every 30 mins, 2½ hrs, US$8. To **Búzios**, from the local bus terminal in the town centre, every hr, US$1. **Útil** to **Belo Horizonte**, US$20. **Unifac** to **Belo Horizonte**, **Juiz da Fora** and

Petrópolis. Macaense runs frequent services to **Macaé**. To **São Paulo**, at 2100, US$22.60.

For the route from Cabo Frio to **Vitória** either take **Macaense** bus to **Macaé** (5¼ hrs), or take **1001** to **Campos** (3½ hrs, US$5.60), and change. **1001** stops in Campos first at the **Shopping Estrada** *rodoviária*, which is the one where the bus connection is made, but it's outside town (US$3 taxi to the centre, or local bus US$0.35). The **1001** then goes on to the local *rodoviária*, closer to the centre, but there are no long-distance services from that terminal. Shopping Estrada *rodoviária* has a tourist office, but no cheap hotels nearby. **Aguia Branca** buses to **Vitória** at 0900 and 1900, US$8.10, 3 hrs 40 mins.

Búzios *p109*
Beach buggies A popular way to get around the cobbled streets of Búzios. Buggy rental is available through most *pousadas* and travel agencies on R das Pedras, or through **Malízia**, T022-2623 2022, www.maliziatour.com.br or Stylus, T022-2623 2780.

Bus The Búzios *rodoviária* is a few blocks' walk from the centre. **1001**, T021-4004 5001, www. autoviacao1001.com.br, to **Rio de Janeiro**, US$18, 3½ hrs (be at the bus terminal 20 mins before departure), 7 departures daily. Buses running between the *rodoviária* Novo Rio in **Rio de Janeiro** and **Cabo Frio** stop at Búzios and are more frequent. Cabo Frio is a 30-min journey from Búzios. Buying the ticket in advance is only recommended on high season and major holidays.

Car By car via the BR-106 takes about 2½ hrs to **Rio de Janeiro** and can take far longer on Sun nights and on Brazilian public holidays.

Inland resorts and coffee towns

The mountain resorts of Petrópolis, Teresópolis and Nova Friburgo are set high in the scenic Serra do Mar behind Rio. All three are lovely mountain retreats with accommodation in charming *fazendas* (coffee estates). The imperial city of Petrópolis retains many of its original buildings and boasts what is perhaps Brazil's finest museum. This is a beautiful area and is becoming increasingly popular for walking, as well as horse riding and other activities. The resorts were originally established because the cool mountain air offered a respite from the heat of Rio and from yellow fever and other diseases that festered in the unhealthy port in the 19th century. They also provided the routes that brought first gold, then coffee from the interior to the coast.

Petrópolis → *For listings, see pages 120-122. Phone code: 024. Population: 290,000.*

Emperor Pedro I, who tired of the sticky summer heat in Rio, longed for a summer palace in the cool of the Atlantic coast mountains but abdicated before he could realize his dream. When the new emperor, Pedro II, took the throne, he soon approved plans presented by the German architect Julius Friedrich Köler for a palace and a new city, to be settled by immigrants. The result was Petrópolis. The city was founded in 1843 and in little over a decade had become a bustling Germanic town and an important imperial summer retreat. The emperor and his family would spend as much as six months of each year here and, as he had his court in tow, Köler was able to construct numerous grand houses and administrative buildings. Many of these still stand – bizarre Rhineland anomalies in a neotropical landscape.

Arriving in Petrópolis

There are buses from the *rodoviária* in Rio every 15 minutes throughout the day and every hour on Sundays. The journey takes about 1½ hours, US$8. Sit on the left-hand side for best views and bring travel sickness pills if you are prone to nausea on winding roads. Return tickets are not available, so buy tickets for the return journey on arrival in Petrópolis. The main **tourist office** ⓘ *Praça da Liberdade, Mon-Sat 0900-1800, Sun 0900-1700*, is at the far southwestern end of Avenida Koeler. It has a list of tourist sights and hotels, a good, free, colour map of the city, and a useful pamphlet in various languages. Some staff are multilingual and very helpful.

Places in Petrópolis

Three rivers dominate the layout of Petrópolis: the **Piabanha**, **Quitandinha** and the **Palatino**. In the historic centre, where most of the sites of tourist interest are to be found, the rivers have been channelled to run down the middle of the main avenues. Their banks are planted with flowering trees and the overall aspect is unusual in Brazil; you quickly get a sense that this was a city built with a specific purpose and at a specific time in Brazil's history.

Petrópolis's main attraction is its imperial palace. The **Museu Imperial** ① *R da Imperatriz 220, T024-2237 8000, Tue-Sun 1100-1730, last entry 1700, US$4, under 6s free, expect long queues on Sun during Easter and high season*, is Brazil's most visited museum and is so well kept you might think the imperial family had left the day before, rather than in 1889. It's modest for an emperor, neoclassical in style and fully furnished, and is worth a visit if just to see the crown jewels of both Pedro I and Pedro II. The palace gardens in front are filled with little fountains, statues and shady benches. Descendants of the original family live in a house behind the palace. Horse-drawn carriages wait to be hired outside the gate; not all the horses are in good shape.

Opposite the Museu Imperial is the handsome **Palácio Amarelo** ① *Praça Visconde de Mauá 89, T024-2291 9200, Tue-Sun 0900-1800, US$1*, built in 1850 as the palace of another Brazilian baron and now the Câmara Municipal (town hall). The twin shady *praças* **dos Expedicionários** and **Dom Pedro II** (which has a pigeon-covered statue of the emperor) lie opposite each other at the

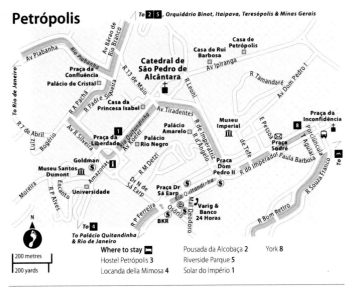

Petrópolis

Where to stay 🛏
Hostel Petrópolis 3
Locanda della Mimosa 4
Pousada da Alcobaça 2
Riverside Parque 5
Solar do Império 1
York 8

junction of Rua do Imperador and Rua da Imperatriz, 100 m south of the Museu Imperial (left as you leave the museum). A small **market** is held here on Sundays and there are a handful of cafés and restaurants.

At the northern end of Rua da Imperatriz (turn right out of the museum and follow the river as it curves left along Avenida Tiradentes) is the Gothic revival **Catedral de São Pedro de Alcântara** ⓘ *R São Pedro de Alcântara 60, T024-2242 4300, Tue-Sun 0800-1200 and 1400-1800, free*, where Emperor Pedro II, his wife Princesa Teresa, Princesa Isabel and Count D'Eu are entombed in mock-European regal marble. This lies at the end of the city's most impressive avenue, **Avenida Koeler**, which is lined with mansions built by the imperial and republican aristocracy. Among them are the neoclassical **Palácio Rio Negro** ⓘ *Av Koeler 255, T024-2246 9380, Mon 1200-1700, Wed-Sun 0930-1700, US$1.50, under 6s free, multilingual guides*, built in 1889 by the Barão do Rio Negro as the summer retreat of Brazilian presidents, and the **Casa da Princesa Isabel** ⓘ *Av Koeler 42, outside visits only*, the former residence of Dom Pedro II's daughter and her husband the Count D'Eu.

Avenida Koeler ends at the **Praça da Liberdade** (formerly known as Praça Rui Barbosa) where there are cafés, goat-drawn carts for children and very photogenic views of the cathedral. A further 100 m west of the *praça* (away from Avenida Koeler) is the **Museu Santos Dumont** ⓘ *R do Encanto 22, T024-2247 3158, Tue-Sun 0930-1700, US$1.50, free for under 6s*. The summer home of Alberto Santos Dumont, who Brazilians claim was the first man to fly an aeroplane, was designed in 1918 as a mock-Alpine chalet. Santos Dumont called it 'the enchanted one', and it is a delightful example of an inventor's house. Steps to the roof lead to an observation point and are carefully designed to allow visitors only to ascend right foot first. His desk doubled up to become his bed. The alcohol-heated shower is said to be the first in Brazil.

The city has a handful of other interesting buildings. The **Casa de Rui Barbosa** ⓘ *Av Ipiranga 405, private residence*, was the home of the Bahian media mogul and writer who was instrumental in abolishing slavery in Brazil. The **Casa de Petrópolis** ⓘ *Av Ipiranga 716, outside visits only*, is a magnificent Gothic folly set in formal French gardens and was built in 1884 by José Tavares Guerra, the grandson of the founder of industrialization in Brazil, the Barão de Mauá. Taking centre stage in the Praça da Confluência is the **Palácio de Cristal**, which was commissioned and built in France following London's great exhibition, when such palaces were all the rage in Europe. It opened to great aplomb, fell into disrepair in the 20th century and is now the home of weekend concerts and shows.

Some 10 km from the centre, on the way to the BR-040 to Rio, is the **Palácio Quitandinha** ⓘ *Av Joaquim Rolla 2, T024-2237 1012, Tue-Sun 0900-1700, US$2.50*, a vast mock-Bavarian edifice that was built in 1944 to be the largest casino in South America. The lake in front of the building is in the shape of

Brazil. Further out of town still is the **Orquidário Binot** ① *R Fernandes Vieira 390, T024-2248 5665, Mon-Fri 0800-1100 and 1300-1600, Sat 0700-1100*. This nursery has one of the best collections of Brazilian orchids in the state and is well worth visiting even if you don't intend to buy.

Teresópolis → *For listings, see pages 120-122. Phone code: 021. Population: 140,000.*

At 910 m this is the highest city in the state of Rio de Janeiro. It was the favourite summer retreat of Empress Teresa Cristina and is named after her. Development in recent years has destroyed some of the city's character, but most visitors use the town as a base for visiting the Serra dos Órgãos, which lie nearby.

Arriving in Teresópolis

Numerous buses run between Teresópolis and Rio's *rodoviária* daily. Eight buses a day run between Teresópolis and Petrópolis. Information is available from the **Secretaria de Turismo** ① *Praça Olímpica, T021-2742 3352, ext 2082*, and **Terminal Turístico Tancredo Neves** ① *Av Rotariana, T021-2642 2094, www. teresopolis.rj.gov.br*, at the entrance to town from Rio. There are very good views of the *serra* from here.

Serra dos Órgãos → *For listings, see pages 120-122.*

These mountains near Teresópolis, named after their strange rock formations, which are said to look like organ pipes, preserve some of the most diverse stretches of Atlantic coast forest in the state of Rio de Janeiro. The flora and fauna (especially birdwatching) here are excellent, as are the walking and rock climbing. The best way to see the park is on foot. A number of trails cut through the forest and head up into the alpine slopes, including the ascent of the **Dedo de Deus** (God's Finger); a precipitous peak that requires some climbing skills. Other trails lead to the highest point in the park, the **Pedra do Sino** (Bell Rock), 2263 m, a three- to four-hour climb up a 14-km path. The west face of this mountain is one of the hardest climbing pitches in Brazil. Other popular walks include the **Pedra do Açu trail** and paths to a variety of anatomically named peaks and outcrops: O Escalavrado (The Scarred One), O Dedo de Nossa Senhora (Our Lady's Finger), A Cabeça de Peixe (Fish Head), A Agulha do Diabo (The Devil's Needle) and A Verruga do Frade (The Friar's Wart).

Arriving in Serra dos Órgãos

If you have a car, a good way to see the park is to do the Rio–Teresópolis–Petrópolis–Rio road circuit, stopping off for walks in the forest. This can be done in a day. The park has two ranger stations, both accessible from the BR-116: the **Sede** ① *headquarters, T021-2642 1070*, is closer to Teresópolis (from town take Avenida Rotariana), while the **Sub-Sede** is just outside the park proper, off the BR-116. By the Sede entrance is the Mirante do Soberbo, with views to the Baía de Guanabara. Both the Sede station and the mirante can be reached on the bus marked 'Mirante do Soberbo', which leaves every half an hour from the Teresópolis *rodoviária* and city centre.

Anyone can enter the park and hike the trails from the Teresópolis gate, but if you intend to climb the Pedra do Sino, you must sign a register (those under 18 must be accompanied by an adult and have permission from the park authorities). Entrance to the park is US$2, with an extra charge for the path to the top of the Pedra do Sino. For information, contact the Rio de Janeiro branch of **Ibama** ① *T021-2231 1772*.

Flora and fauna

The park belongs to the threatened Mata Atlântica coastal rainforest, designated by **Conservation International** as a global biodiversity hot spot and the preserve of what are probably the richest habitats in South America outside the Amazonian cloudforests. There are 20- to 30-m-high trees, such as *paineiras* (floss-silk tree), *ipês* and *cedros*, rising above palms, bamboos and other smaller trees. Flowers include begonias, bromeliads, orchids and *quaresmeiras* (glorybushes). The park is home to numerous rare and endemic birds including cotingas, the rarest of which is the grey-winged cotinga, guans, tanagers, berryeaters and trogons. Mammals include titi and capuchin monkeys, all of the neo-tropical rainforest cats including jaguar and oceleot, tapir and white collared peccary. Reptiles include the *sapo-pulga* (flea-toad), which at 10 mm long vies with the Cuban pygmy frog as the smallest amphibian in the world.

Inland resorts and coffee towns listings

For hotel and restaurant price codes and other relevant information, see pages 9-13.

💬 Where to stay

Petrópolis *p116, map p117*
Good budget accommodation is hard to find, but bargaining is possible Mon-Fri.

$$$$ Locanda della Mimosa,
Alameda das Mimosas, Vale Florido, T024-2233 5405, www.locanda. com.br. A 6-room *pousada* in a terracotta Palladian villa in the mountains near town, overlooking a little pool. The owner is one of the finest chefs in Brazil, see page 121.
$$$$ Pousada da Alcobaça,
R Agostinho Goulão 298, Correas,

T024-2221 1240, www.pousada daalcobaca.com.br. In the **Roteiros de Charme** group. Delightful, family-run large country house set in flower-filled gardens leading down to a river, with pool and sauna.

$$$$ Solar do Império, Av Koeler 376, T024-2103 3000, www.solardoimperio. com.br. A luxury boutique hotel with period furniture in a converted mansion opposite the Palácio Rio Negro. Excellent spa and restaurant.

$$$ Riverside Parque, R Hermogéneo Silva 522, Retiro, 5 mins from the centre, T024-2246 9850, www.hoteis-riverside.com.br. Mock-colonial hotel with a nice outdoor pool set in attractive gardens with views of the surrounding countryside. The helpful owner can arrange tours.

$$ Hostel Petrópolis, R Santos Dumont 345, Centro, T024-2237 3811, www.hostel petropolisoficial.com.br. Well-kept and well-run hostel situated in a brightly painted red townhouse conveniently located in the city centre.

$$ York, R do Imperador 78, near the *rodoviária*, T024-2243 2662, www.hotelyork.com.br. Convenient package-tour hotel with faded 1980s rooms, decent breakfast.

Teresópolis *p119*

Many cheap hotels on R Delfim Moreira.

$$$$ Fazenda Rosa dos Ventos, Km 22 on the road to Nova Friburgo, T021-2644 9900, www.hotelrosados ventos.com.br. Part of the **Roteiros de Charme** chain. One of the best hotels in inland Rio with a range of chalets in 1 million sq m of private forest and with wonderful views. Excellent restaurant.

$ Recanto do Lord Hostel, R Luiza Pereira Soares 109, Centro-Artistas, T021-2742 5586, www.teresopolis hostel.com.br. Family-oriented hostel with rooms and dorms, kitchen, cable TV and barbecue area. Camping is permitted beside the hostel.

Serra dos Órgãos *p119*

Ibama has some hostels, US$5 full board, or US$3 first night, US$2 thereafter, a bit rough.

$$$$ Reserva Ecológica de Guapi Assu (REGUA), Cachoeiras de Macacu-RJ, T021-2745 3998, www.regua.co.uk. A British-run conservation NGO and ecotourism project focused on a large main house with several rooms, set in primary rainforest. Expert guided walks into the reserve, in one of the richest areas in the state for birds, mammals and orchids.

$$$$ Serra dos Tucanos, Caixa Postal 98125, Cachoeiras do Macacu, T021-2649 1557, www.serrados tucanos.com.br. One of the best wildlife and birdwatching lodges in Brazil with excellent guiding, equipment and accommodation in a comfortable lodge set in the Atlantic coastal rainforest.

🍴 Restaurants

Petrópolis *p116, map p117*

Bakeries and cheap eateries by the *rodoviária*

$$$ Locanda della Mimosa, Alameda das Mimosas, Vale Florido, T024-2233 5405, www.locanda. com.br. One of the best restaurants in Brazil, offering fusion cooking with a focus on game. Danio Braga was 4 times *Quatro Rodas* chef of the year. The 3000-bottle wine cellar includes heavyweights like 1990 Château Haut-Brion.

○ What to do

Petrópolis *p116, map p117*
Rio Serra, T024-2235 7607, www.rioserra.com.br/trekking. Horse riding, trekking, whitewater rafting and a range of trips into the scenic mountain area, multilingual guides.
Roz Brazil, T024-9257 0236, www.rozbrazil.com. Some of the best drive and light walk tours around Petrópolis, Teresópolis and the Serra dos Órgãos with British Brazilian Rosa Thompson, who has been living in the area for decades. Pick-ups from Rio.

Serra dos Órgãos *p119*
Tours are available through the tourist office or the **IYHA Recanto do Lord** in Teresópolis. See also **Roz Brazil**, above.
Lazer Tours, T024-2742 7616. Tours of the park are offered by Francisco (find him at the grocery shop on R Sloper 1). Recommended.

○ Transport

Petrópolis *p116, map p117*
Bus Buses run to **Rio de Janeiro** every 30 mins throughout the day (US$10), Sun every hour, 1½ hrs, sit on the right-hand side for best views, www.unica-facil.com.br. Ordinary buses arrive in Rio at the *rodoviária*; a/c buses run hourly and arrive at Av Nilo Peçanha, US$4. Book your return journey as soon as you arrive in Petrópolis. Bus to **Niterói**, US$11; to **Cabo Frio**, US$26. To **Teresópolis**, 8 a day, US$3. To **São Paulo** daily at 2330.

Teresópolis *p119*
Bus The *rodoviária* is at R 1 de Maio 100. Buses to **Rio de Janeiro** Novo Rio *rodoviária* every 30 mins. Book your return journey as soon as you arrive in Teresópolis. Fare US$3.60. From Teresópolis to **Petrópolis**, 8 a day, US$3.

West of Rio de Janeiro

Towns to the west of Rio are mostly spread along the ugly Rio–São Paulo motorway known as the Via Dutra. None are appealing. But the mountains that watch over them preserve important tracts of Atlantic coast rainforest, particularly around Itatiaia. This is one of the best places close to Rio for seeing wild animals and virgin rainforest and is the country's oldest protected area. The little mock-Alpine resort of Visconde de Mauá sits in the same mountain chain a little further towards São Paulo, although the forest here is less well preserved.

Parque Nacional de Itatiaia → *For listings, see pages 126-127.*

Deep valleys shrouded in pristine rainforest hiding rocky clear-water rivers and icy waterfalls. Little winding trails through a whole swathe of different ecosystems, watched over by some of world's rarest birds and mammals. Hotels and guesthouses to suit all budgets from which to explore them. And all within easy reach of Rio or São Paulo.

Itatiaia is a must for those who wish to see Brazilian forest and animals and have a restricted itinerary or limited time. This 30,000-ha mountainous park is Brazil's oldest. It was founded in 1937 to protect Atlantic coast rainforest in the Serra de Mantiqueira mountains, and important species still find a haven here, including jaguars and pumas, brown capuchin and black-faced titi monkeys. This is good hiking country with walks through subtropical and temperate forests, grasslands and *paramo* to a few peaks just under 3000 m. The best trails head for Pedra de Taruga, Pedra de Maçã and the Poranga and Véu de Noiva waterfalls. The Pico das Agulhas Negras and Serra das Prateleiras (up to 2540 m) offer good rock climbing. There is a **Museu de História Natural** ① *Tue-Sun 1000-1600*, near the park headquarters with a depressing display of stuffed animals from the 1940s.

Arriving in Parque Nacional de Itatiaia
Getting there and around Itatiaia lies just off the main São Paulo–Rio highway, the Dutra. A bus marked '504 Circular' runs from Itatiaia town run four times a day (variable hours) to the park, calling at the hotels in town. The bus can also be caught at Resende, at the crossroads before Itatiaia. Tickets are sold at a booth in the large bar in the middle of Itatiaia main street.

The alternative option involves adding another 10 to 15 km on to your journey depending on where you are staying in town. There is one bus that goes to the park used mostly by the park employees. The bus leaves at 0700 from the road that leads to the park's gate. It takes about 30 minutes and costs about US$1.50; stay in the bus until the last stop. Check out the return time in advance. There are also guides that provide their own transport. A local guide for this trek costs US$15 per person.

The best way to see the park is to hire a car or with a tour operator. There is only one way into the park from Itatiaia town and one main road within it – which forks off to the various hotels, all of which are signposted. **Ralph Salgueiro** ① *T024-3351 1823/024-9952 5962, www.ecoralph.com*, offers general tours. **Edson Endrigo** ① *www.avesfoto.com.br*, is one of Brazil's foremost birding guides and offers wildlife tours in Itatiaia and throughout Brazil. English spoken.

Tourist information Entry per day is US$10 per car. Basic accommodation in cabins and dormitories is available in the village strung along the road leading to the park. There are some delightful options inside the park but they are more expensive. Avoid weekends and Brazilian holidays if wildlife watching is a priority. Information and maps can be obtained at the **Administração do Parque Nacional de Itatiaia (park office)** ① *Estrada Parque Km 8.5, www.ibama. gov.br/parna_itatiaia*. Information can also be obtained from **Ibama** ① *T024-33521461 for the local headquarters, or T021-3224 6463 for the Rio de Janeiro state department*. The **Administração do Parque Nacional de Itatiaia** operates a refuge in the park, which acts as a starting point for climbs and treks. Information on trekking can be obtained from **Clube Excursionista Brasileiro** ① *Av Almirante Barroso 2, 8th floor, Rio de Janeiro, T021-2252 9844, www.ceb.org.br*.

Flora and fauna
The park is particularly good for birds. It has a list of more than 350 species with scores of spectacular tanagers, hummingbirds (including the ultra-rare Brazilian ruby, with emerald wings and a dazzling red chest), cotingas (included the black and gold cotinga, which as far as we are aware has never been photographed) and manakins. Guans squawk and flap right next to the park roads.

The vegetation is stratified by altitude so that the plateau at 800-1100 m is covered by forest, ferns and flowering plants (such as orchids, bromeliads, begonias), giving way on the higher escarpments to pines and bushes. Higher still, over 1900 m, the distinctive rocky landscape has low bushes and grasses, isolated trees and unique plants adapted to high winds and strong sun. There is also a great variety of lichens.

Places and hikes in Parque Nacional de Itatiaia

The park also offers excellent trail walking. There are peaks with magnificent views out over the Atlantic coastal forest and the Rio de Janeiro coastline and a series of beautiful waterfalls; many of which are easily accessible from the park road. The trails, most of which begin just behind the Hotel Simon or around the visitor centre, cut through the forest, bushland and up into the alpine paramo, dotted with giant granite boulders. The views from here are breathtaking. Walking the trails can be one of the best ways of seeing a good cross section of the habitats and their flora and fauna. Be sure to take plenty of water, repellent and a fleece for the higher areas. Temperatures can drop well below 0°C in the winter. Information on the trails is available from the visitor centre, which holds maps and gives directions to all the trail heads (though English is poor). The adjacent museum has a collection of stuffed animals, all of which exist in fully animated form in the park itself.

Maçico das Prateleiras peak, one of the highest in the park (2548 m) is a full day's walk for experienced hikers. When there is no mist the views are magnificent. To get there, take the trail from Abrigo Rebouças mountain lodge, reached from the BR354 road that heads north out of Engenheiro Passos – the next town beyond Itatiaia on BR116 (The Dutra). From here it is around 1½ hours. **Pico das Agulhas Negras** is the highest point in the park (2787 m) and is reached via the same route as Maçico das Prateleiras, but with a turn to the east at the Abrigo Rebouças (instead of west). The upper reaches are only accessible with a rope and moderate climbing experience. This is another full day's walk. **Tres Picos** is a six-hour walk, leaving from a trail signposted off to the right, about 3 km beyond the visitor centre. It is one of the best for a glimpse of the park's various habitats. The first half of the trail is fairly gentle, but after about an hour the path gets progressively steep. An hour or so beyond the steep trail is the **Rio Bonito** – a great place for a break, where there is a beautiful waterfall for swimming and refreshment. There are wonderful views from the top, which is another 45 minutes further on. The **Piscina do Maromba** is a natural pool formed by the Rio Campo Belo and situated at 1100 m. It's one of the most refreshing places to swim in the park – although most Brazilians find it far too cold. Trails leave for here from behind Hotel Simon.

There are a number of **waterfalls** in the park; most of which have pools where you can swim. The most accessible is **Cachoeira Poranga** – left off the park road about 3.5 km beyond the visitor centre. **Itaporani** and **Véu da Noiva** are reached by a path just beyond the Poranga trail; which leaves from next to the road bridge and divides after about 1 km – left for Véu da Noiva, right for Itaporani.

Engenheiro Passos → *Phone code: 024. Population: 3500.*
Further along the Dutra highway (186 km from Rio) is the small town of
Engenheiro Passos, from which a road (BR-354) leads to São Lourenço and
Caxambu in Minas Gerais. By turning off this road at the Registro Pass (1670 m)
on the Rio–Minas border, you can reach the **Pico das Agulhas Negras**. The
mountain can be climbed from this side from the **Abrigo Rebouças** refuge at
2350 m, which is manned all year round; US$2.50 per night, take your own food.

West of Rio de Janeiro listings

*For hotel and restaurant price codes and other
relevant information, see pages 9-13.*

● Where to stay

Parque Nacional de Itatiaia *p123*
$$$ Hotel Donati, T024-3352 1110,
www.hoteldonati.com.br. One of
the most delightful hotels in the
country – mock-Swiss chalets and
rooms, set in tropical gardens visited
by animals every night and early
morning. A series of trails leads off
from the main building and the
hotel can organize professional
birding guides. Decent restaurant
and 2 pools. Highly recommended.
$$ Hotel do Ypê, T024-3352 7453,
www.hoteldoype.com.br. Inside the
park with sauna and heated pool.
**$$ Pousada Aldeia dos
Passaros**, T024-3352 1152, www.
aldeiadospassaros.com. 10 chalets
with fireplaces and balconies in
secondary forest overlooking a
stream in the lower reaches of
the park. Great breakfasts, good off-
season rates and a riverside sauna.
$$ Pousada Country, Estrada do
Parque Nacional 848, T024-3352
1433, www.pousadacountry.com.br.

A bit cheaper but outside the park
on the paved access road. There are a
couple of other smaller hotels and a
restaurant close by.
$$ Pousada Esmeralda, Estrada
do Parque, T024-3352 1643, www.
pousadaesmeralda.com.br. Very
comfortable chalets set around
a lake in a lawned garden and
furnished with chunky wooden
beds, tables and chests of drawers
and warmed by log fires. Be sure to
book a table for a candlelit dinner.
$ Ypê Amarelo, R João Maurício
Macedo Costa 352, Campo Alegre,
T024-3352 1232, www.pousadaype
amarelo.com.br. **IYHA** youth hostel
with annexes set in an attractive
garden visited by hummingbirds.

Engenheiro Passos *p126*
Around Engenheiro Passos there are
many *fazenda* hotels.
$$$$ Hotel Fazenda 3 Pinheiros,
Caxambu, Km 23, T024-2108 1000,
www.3pinheiros.com.br. Large
resort charging all inclusive rates
with 3 meals provided. Special
rates for trekkers that only sleep
over are negotiable.

● What to do

Parque Nacional de Itatiaia *p123*
Ralph Salgueiro, T024-3351 1823,
www.ecoralph.com; and **Edson
Endrigo**, T024-3742 8374, www.
avesfoto.com.br, offer birdwatching
trips in Itatiaia and throughout Brazil,
English spoken.

Engenheiro Passos *p126*
Levy, T024-3352 6097, T024-8812
0006 (mob), www.levyecologico.
com.br. Experienced guide that takes
trekking groups to the high region of
Itatiaia Park. Portuguese only.

Miguel, T024-3360 5224, T024-7834
2128 (mob). Local guide know the
region really well. Portuguese only.

● Transport

Parque Nacional de Itatiaia *p123*
Bus Bus '504 Circular' to/from **Itatiaia
town** 4 times daily, picks up from
Hotel Simon in the park and stops
at **Resende** (at the crossroads before
Itatiaia) and hotels in town.

Itatiaia town has bus connections
with **São Paulo** and **Rio de Janeiro**
and it's possible to buy through tickets
from the middle of the main street.

Costa Verde

The Rio de Janeiro–Santos section of the BR-101 is one of the world's most beautiful highways, hugging the forested and hilly Costa Verde southwest of Rio. The Serra do Mar mountains plunge down to the sea in a series of spurs that disappear into the Atlantic to reappear as a cluster of islands offshore. The most beautiful of these is Ilha Grande: an 80,000-ha mountain ridge covered in rainforest and fringed with wonderful beaches. Beyond Ilha Grande, further down the coast towards São Paulo, is one of Brazil's prettiest colonial towns, Paraty, which sits surrounded by long white beaches in front of a glorious bay of islands. Seen from the harbour in the morning light, this is one of Brazil's most photographed sights.

Arriving on the Costa Verde

The BR-101 is paved all the way to Santos, which has good links with São Paulo. Buses from Rio run to Angra dos Reis, Paraty, Ubatuba, Caraguatatuba and São Sebastião, where it may be necessary to change for Santos or São Paulo. Hotels and *pousadas* have sprung up all along the road, as have expensive housing developments, though these have not spoiled the views. The drive from Rio to Paraty should take four hours, but it would be better to break the journey and enjoy some of the attractions. The coast road has lots of twists and turns so, if prone to motion sickness, get a seat at the front of the bus to make the most of the views.

Angra dos Reis and around → *For listings, see pages 136-144. Phone code: 024.*

The vast bay of Angra dos Reis is studded with more lush islands than there are days in the year. Some are the private playgrounds of Carioca playboys. Others are media islands, owned by magazines devoted to the cult of the Brazilian celebrity, and permanently twinkling with camera flashes. A few are thronged with bikinis and board shorts in high season and pulsate to *forró* and samba beats. And many are as wild and unspoilt as they were when the Portuguese arrived 500 years ago. Yachts and speedboats flit across the bay, ferrying their bronzed and smiling cargo between the islands and beaches. In between, they dock at floating bars and restaurants for an icy caipirinha or catch of the day, and at night to dance or be lulled by the gentle sound of bossa nova.

Angra town itself is scruffy and down at heel – little more than a jumping-off point to the private islands and to Ilha Grande – but it's an increasingly popular destination for international travellers. This is a result of the migration of the wealthy out of Rio and their acquisition of beaches and property from the local fishermen, whose families now live in the *favelas* that encrust the surrounding hills.

Angra was once a pretty colonial town like Paraty further along the coast, and several buildings remain from its heyday. Of particular note are the church and convent of **Nossa Senhora do Carmo**, built in 1593 on Praça General Osório, the **Igreja Matriz de Nossa Senhora da Conceição** (1626) in the centre of town and the church and convent of **São Bernardino de Sena** (1758-1763) on the Morro do Santo Antônio. On the Largo da Lapa is the church of **Nossa Senhora da Lapa da Boa Morte** (1752) and a **Museum of Sacred Art** ① *Thu-Sun 1000-1200, 1400-1800*.

On the Península de Angra, west of the town, is the **Praia do Bonfim**, a popular beach; offshore is the island of the same name, on which the **hermitage of Senhor do Bonfim** (1780) is located. Some 15 km east are the ruins of the **Jacuecanga seminary** (1797).

Angra is connected to Rio and Paraty by regular buses, to Ilha Grande by ferry and fishing boat, and to Ilha do Gipóia by fishing boat. The **tourist office** ① *Av Julio Maria, T024-3365 2041, www.angra-dos-reis.com, www.angra.rj.gov.br*, is just behind the Cais de Santa Luiza quay. The websites have more information than the office.

Ilha Grande → *For listings, see pages 136-144. Phone code: 021.*

Ilha Grande is a mountain ridge covered in tropical forest protruding from the emerald sea and fringed by some of the world's most beautiful beaches. There are no cars and no roads, just trails through the forest, so the island is still relatively undeveloped. With luck it will remain so, as much of Ilha Grande forms part of a state park and biological reserve, and cannot even be visited.

That the island has so much forest is largely a fluke of history. The island was a notorious pirate lair in the 16th and 17th centuries and then a landing port for slaves. By the 20th century it was the site of an infamous prison for the country's most notorious criminals, including the writer Graciliano Ramos, whose *Memórias do Cárcere* relate his experiences. The prison closed in 1994 and is now overgrown. Since then Ilha Grande has been a well-kept Brazilian secret, and is gradually becoming part of the international backpacker circuit.

Arriving in Ihla Grande

Fishing boats and ferries (Barcas SA ① *T021-2533 7524*), leave from Angra dos Reis and Mangaratiba taking two hours or so to reach Vila do Abraão, the island's only real village. From Angra they only leave in the morning and early afternoon and must be chartered (US$60-100 per boat; it is usually possible to get a group together in high season). The weather is best from March to June and the island is overrun during the Christmas, New Year and Carnaval periods. There is a helpful **tourist office** on the jetty at Abraão. Further information and pictures can be found at www.ilhagrande.com. Be wary of undercover police searching for backpackers smoking cannabis on Ilha Grande's beaches.

Beaches and walks

The beach at **Abraão** may look beautiful to new arrivals but those further afield are far more spectacular. The two most famous are: **Lopes Mendes**, a long stretch of sand on the eastern (ocean side) backed by flatlands and patchy forest; and **Aventureiro**, fringed by coconut palms and tropical forest, its powder-fine sand pocked with boulders and washed by a transparent aquamarine sea. Lopes Mendes is two hours' walk from Abraão. Aventureiro is over six hours, but it can be reached by boat. A few fishermen's huts and *barracas* provide food and accommodation here but there is no camping. Good beaches closer to Abraão include the half-moon bay at **Abraãoozinho** (15 minutes' walk) and **Grande das Palmas**, which has a delightful tiny whitewashed chapel (one hour 20 minutes' walk). Both lie east of the town past **Hotel Sagu**. There are boat trips to **Lagoa Azul**, with crystal-clear water and reasonable snorkelling, **Freguesia de Santana** and **Saco do Céu**.

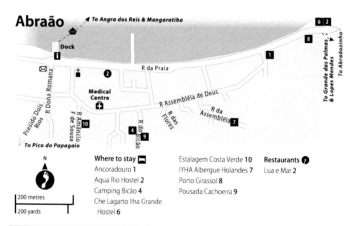

Abraão   ◀ To Angra dos Reis & Mangaratiba

Dock

R da Praia

R Assembléia de Deus

R da Assembléia

Medical Centre

Presido Dois Rios

R Dona Romana

R Amâncio F de Souza

R do Bicão

R das Flores

To Pico do Papagaio

To Grande das Palmas & Lopes Mendes

To Abraãozinho

N

200 metres
200 yards

Where to stay
Ancoradouro 1
Aqua Rio Hostel 2
Camping Bicão 4
Che Lagarto Ilha Grande
　Hostel 6

Estalagem Costa Verde 10
IYHA Albergue Holandes 7
Porto Girassol 8
Pousada Cachoeira 9

Restaurants
Lua e Mar 2

The caiçaras

Brazilians of mixed Indian, African and Portuguese race living on the coast and leading traditional lives fishing and hunting are known as *caiçaras*. Until the 1970s almost all the beaches and islands between Rio de Janeiro and Santos were home to caiçara communities. But then the Rio to Santos main highway was constructed and floods of visitors began to pour in. With them came developments – for luxury private houses, hotels and condominiums like Laranjeiras – which is home to members of Brazil's wealthy and allegedly highly corrupt elite. *Caiçara* communities were bought off for pittance or forced from their land with threats of violence or even death. And an entire way of life and knowledge of the Atlantic coast forest, strongly rooted in indigenous traditions is in danger of being entirely lost. All the *favelas* in Angra dos Reis bear the name of a different beach on Ilha Grande or the beaches and islands around the bay. Nowadays there are *caiçara* communities only on a few isolated stretches between Rio and Santos – like the Ponta da Joatinga peninsula south of Paraty and Aventureiros beach in Ilha Grande. Many think that carefully managed, sensitive ecotourism will help protect them and spread the story of their plight, which is little known even within Brazil.

There are a couple of good treks over the mountains to **Dois Rios**, where the old jail was situated. There is still a settlement of former prison guards here who have nowhere to go. The walk is about 13 km each way, takes about three hours and affords beautiful scenery and superb views. Another three-hour hike is to **Pico do Papagaio** (980 m) through forest; it's a steep climb for which a guide is essential, however, the view from the top is breathtaking. **Pico da Pedra d'Água** (1031 m) can also be climbed.

Paraty → *For listings, see pages 136-144. Phone code: 024. Population: 30,000.*

Paraty is one of Brazil's prettiest colonial towns and one of Rio de Janeiro state's most popular tourist destinations. It is at its most captivating at dawn, when all but the dogs and chickens are sleeping. As the sun peeps over the horizon the little rectilinear streets are infused with a rich golden light, which warms the whitewash and brilliant blue-and-yellow window frames of the colonial townhouses and the façades of the Manueline churches. Brightly coloured fishing boats bob up and down in the water in the foreground and behind the town the deep green of the rainforest-covered mountains of the Serra da Bocaina sit shrouded in their self-generated wispy cloud. The town was founded in the 17th century as a gold port and most of its historic buildings date from this period.

At the weekend Paraty buzzes with tourists who browse in the little boutiques and art galleries or buy souvenirs from the Guarani who proffer their wares on the cobbles. At night they fill the little bars and restaurants, many of which, like the *pousadas*, are owned by the bevy of expat Europeans who have found their haven in Paraty and who are determined to preserve its charm. During the week, especially off season, the town is quiet and intimate, its atmosphere as yet unspoilt by the increasing numbers of independent travellers.

The town's environs are as beautiful as Paraty itself. Just a few kilometres away lie the forests of the **Ponta do Juatinga Peninsula**, fringed by wonderful beaches, washed by little waterfalls and still home to communities of Caiçara fishermen who live much as they have done for centuries. Islands pepper the bay, some of them home to ultra-rare animals such as the tiny golden lion tamarin monkey, which is found nowhere else. The best way to visit these destinations is on a boat trip with one of the town's fishermen from the quay.

Arriving in Paraty

The *rodoviária* is at the corner of Rua Jango Padua and Rua da Floresta. There are direct bus connections with Rio and São Paulo several times daily, and with a number of destinations along the coast. Taxis charge a set rate of US$4 from the bus station to the historic centre, which is pedestrianized and easily negotiable on foot. Staff at the **Centro de Informações Turísticas** ① *Av Roberto Silveira, near the entrance to the historic centre, T024-3371 1266*, are friendly and helpful and some speak English. There is a good town map in the *Welcome to Paraty* brochure, www.eco-paraty.com. More information is available at www.paraty.com.br. The wettest months are January, February, June and July. In spring, the streets in the colonial centre may flood, but the houses remain above the waterline. ►► *See Transport, page 143.*

Places in Paraty

In keeping with all Brazilian colonial towns, Paraty's churches were built according to social status and race. There are four churches in the town, one for the 'freed coloured men', one for the blacks and two for the whites. **Santa Rita** (1722), built by the 'freed coloured men' in elegant Brazilian baroque, faces the bay and the port. It is probably the most famous picture postcard image of Paraty and houses a small **Museum of Sacred Art** ① *Wed-Sun 0900-1200, 1300-1800, US$1.* **Nossa Senhora do Rosário e São Benedito** ① *R do Comércio, Tue 0900-1200* (1725, rebuilt 1757), built by black slaves, is small and simple; the slaves were unable to raise the funds to construct an elaborate building. **Nossa Senhora dos Remédios** ① *Mon, Wed, Fri, Sat 0900-1200, Sun 0900-1500,* is the town's parish church, the biggest in Paraty. It was started in 1787 but construction continued until 1873. The church was never completely finished as it was built on unstable ground; the architects decided not to add weight to the structure by putting up the towers. The façade is leaning to the left, which is clear from the three doors (only the one on the right has a step). Built with donations from the whites, it is rumoured that Dona Geralda Maria da Silva contributed gold from a pirate's hoard found buried on the beach. **Capela de Nossa Senhora das Dores** ① *Thu 0900-1200* (1800), is a chapel facing the sea. It was used mainly by wealthy 19th-century whites.

There is a great deal of distinguished Portuguese colonial architecture in delightful settings. **Rua do Comércio** is the main street in the historic centre. It was here that the prominent traders lived, the two-storey houses having the commercial establishments on the ground floor and the residences above. Today the houses are occupied by restaurants, *pousadas* and tourist shops.

The **Casa da Cadeia**, close to Santa Rita Church, is the former jail, complete with iron grilles in the windows and doors. It is now a public library and art gallery.

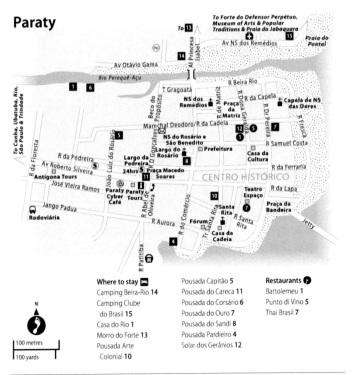

Paraty

Where to stay 🛏
Camping Beira-Rio **14**
Camping Clube
  do Brasil **15**
Casa do Rio **1**
Morro do Forte **13**
Pousada Arte
  Colonial **10**

Pousada Capitão **5**
Pousada do Careca **11**
Pousada do Corsário **6**
Pousada do Ouro **7**
Pousada do Sandi **8**
Pousada Pardieiro **4**
Solar dos Gerânios **12**

Restaurants 🍴
Bartolemeu **1**
Punto di Vino **5**
Thai Brasil **7**

On the northern headland is a small fort, **Forte do Defensor Perpétuo**, built in 1822, whose cannon and thick ruined walls can be seen. From the fort there are good views of the sea and the roofs of the town. It's about 15 minutes' walk from the centre. To get there, cross the Rio Perequê Açu by the bridge at the end of the Rua do Comércio; climb the small hill, which has some attractive *pousadas* and a cemetery, and follow the signs. Also here is the **Museum of Arts and Popular Traditions** ① *Wed-Sun*, in a colonial-style building. It contains carved wooden canoes, musical instruments, fishing gear and other items from local communities. On the headland is the gunpowder store and enormous hemispherical iron pans that were used for extracting whale oil, which was used for lamps and to mix with sand and cement for building.

Boat trips and beaches

The most popular trip, and highly recommended, is a five-hour **schooner tour** around the bay for swimming (US$15, lunch is an optional extra). Smaller boats are available for US$10 an hour or US$20 for three hours. Many beautiful beaches are visited.

Praia do Pontal is the town beach, five minutes' walk from the historic centre: cross the bridge and turn right along the river. The water and sand are not very clean but the handful of *barracas* under the trees are a nice place to hang out. **Praia do Jabaquara** is about 20 minutes away on foot: cross the bridge and continue straight up the hill. There are a few *barracas* here and the sand is cleaner, but the water tends to be muddy.

There are other beaches further from town, many of which make worthwhile excursions. Scruffy **Boa Vista** is just south of town and beyond this (reachable only by boat) are, in order, the long, broad and clean stretches of **Praia da Conçeicao**, **Praia Vermelha** and **Praia da Lula**, all of which have simple restaurants and are backed by forest and washed by gentle waves. The **Saco da Velha**, further south still, is small and intimate, protected by an island and surrounded by rainforested slopes.

The small town of **Paraty Mirím**, is 17 km away and has a vast sweeping beach with a Manueline church built on the sand and some ruined colonial buildings. It is reached by boat or by four buses a day (three on Sunday) and has simple restaurants and places to camp. Fishing boats leave from here for other islands and beaches including the **Praia do Pouso da Cajaíba**, which has lodgings of the same name, and the spectacular sweep at **Martim do Sá**. The **Saco do Mamanguá** is a long sleeve of water that separates the Ponta da Juatinga and Paraty Mirím, which has good snorkelling.

Caminho do Ouro (Gold Trail) → *www.caminhodoouro.com.br.*

This partly cobbled trail through the mountains was built by slaves in the 18th century to bring gold down from Ouro Preto before transporting it to Portugal.

Recently restored, it can be visited, along with the ruins of a toll house, on foot or horseback as a day trip. Tours leave at 1000 from the **Teatro Espaço** ① *R Dona Geralda 327, T024-3371 1575.*

There are several *cachoeiras* (waterfalls) in the area, such as the **Cachoeira da Penha**, near the church of the same name. It is 10 km from town on the road to Cunha; take a local bus from the *rodoviária*, US$1, there are good mountain views on the way. The tourist office and travel agencies have details on the waterfalls and hikes.

A recommended excursion is to **Fazenda Murycana** ① *T024-3371 3930 for tours and information,* an old sugar estate and 17th-century *cachaça* distillery with original house and waterwheel. You can taste and buy the different types of *cachaça*; some are aged in oak barrels for 12 years. Try the *cachaça com cravo e canela* (with clove and cinnamon). There is an excellent restaurant and horse riding is available but English is not spoken by the employees. Mosquitoes can be a problem at the *fazenda*, take repellent and don't wear shorts. To get there, take a 'Penha/Ponte Branca' bus from the *rodoviária*, four a day; alight where it crosses a small white bridge and then walk 10 minutes along a signed, unpaved road. There is a good chance of hitching a lift back to Paraty.

Trindade → *For listings, see pages 136-144.*

Ramshackle little Trindade (pronounced *Tringdajee*) may not be as beautiful in its own right as Paraty but its setting, sandwiched between rainforested slopes and emerald sea, is equally spectacular. And, unlike Paraty, it has a long, broad beach. The town has long been a favourite hang-out for young middle-class surf hippies from São Paulo and Rio, who come here in droves during the holiday period. It is now also finding its place on the international backpacker circuit and it's easy to see why. The beach is spectacular, the *pousadas* and restaurants cheap and cheerful, and there are a number of campsites. Sadly there is no sewage treatment and when the town is full, foul black water flows onto the sand. There are plenty of unprepossessing restaurants along the town's main drag, **Avenida Principal**. All serve the usual 'beans and rice and chips' combinations. Avoid coming here during Christmas, New Year, Carnaval and Easter.

Arriving in Trindade Trindade is 30 km south of Paraty. It is reached by a steep, winding 7-km road branching off the Rio–Santos road (BR-101). Buses that run between Paraty and Ubatuba all pass the turning to Trindade and will drop you or pick you up here. Ask for 'Patrimonio' or 'Estrada para Trindade'. In high season there are vans from here to Trindade (US$2). In low season you'll have to hitch or walk; cars pass regularly. Be wary of carrying any drugs – the police at the turn-off post are very vigilant and searches are frequent. **Tourist information** is available at the booth at the entrance to town (no English spoken) or through the Paraty website, www.paraty.com.br and tourist office. Trindade has no banks.

Around Trindade

Beyond Trindade and the upmarket condominium at **Laranjeiras** there is a series of beaches. **Sono** is a long, sweeping stretch of sand backed by *barracas*, some of which have accommodation to rent. Sanitation is a problem, however. **Ponta Negra** is a little *caiçara* village, beautifully situated in a cove between rocky headlands. It has its own beach, simple but elegant homestay accommodation, fishing-boat trips and organized treks into the surrounding forest, which is rich in birdlife and full of waterfalls. It is possible to climb to the highest peak on the peninsula for views out over the Paraty area. The community is traditional and conservative; visits should be arranged in advance through village leaders. ▸ *See Where to stay, page 140.*

Arriving in Sono and Ponta Negra Sono and Ponta Negra are reached from the Sono trailhead, which lies at the end of the bus route to Trindade/Laranjeiras. The path is easy to find and follow. Allow 1½ hours for Sono and three hours for Ponta Negra. There are several buses a day to Trindade and the trailhead from Paraty. ▸ *See Transport, page 143.*

Costa Verde listings

For hotel and restaurant price codes and other relevant information, see pages 9-13.

◌ Where to stay

Angra dos Reis and around *p128*
Only stay in Angra town if you miss your bus or boat. There are a few cheap hotels near the port and main *praça*.
$$$$ Pestana, Estr do Contorno 3700, Km 13, T024-3367 2754, www.pestanahotels.com.br. A range of bungalows on a forested hillside overlooking an emerald-green sea. Very pretty, peaceful and secluded.

$$ Caribe, R de Conceição 255, T024-3365 0033, www.angra2reis.com.br/caribe. Central and well kept with rather cheesy 1970s rooms in a tower near the centre.

Ilha Grande *p129*
Accommodation on the island is in *pousadas* at **Vila do Abraão** or camping elsewhere. It is possible to hire a fisherman's cottage on **Aventureiro Beach**, which can be reached on the *Maria Isabel* or *Mestre Ernani* boats (T021-3361 9895 or T021-9269 5877) that leave from the quay in front of the BR petrol station

in Angra dos Reis. Alternatively boats can be chartered direct from Angra dos Reis (2-3 hrs). There's a handful of upmarket options in isolated locations reachable only by boat. **Hidden Pousadas Brazil**, www.hidden pousadasbrazil.com, offers some of the best accommodation on Ilha Grande, both in Abraão and on the quieter beaches.

Abraão *p130, map p130*
Reservations are only necessary in peak season or on holiday weekends.
$$$ Aratinga Inn, Vila do Abraão, www.aratingailhagrande.com.br, or through **Hidden Pousadas**. The simple furnishing in the rooms (there's little more than a bed and a table) are more than made up for by the lovely location, nestled in a lush tropical garden dotted with boulders right under the brow of Papagaio peak, and the excellent service which includes Anglo-Australian afternoon tea.
$$$ Estrela da Ilha, Praia Pequena da Freguesia de Santana, www. estreladailha.com, or through **Hidden Pousadas**. Isolated location but magnificent ocean views from airy, rustic but romantic chunky wood rooms and easy access to snorkelling sites and broad sandy beaches. On-site yoga and healthy food; full board.
$$$-$$ Pousada Manaca, Praia do Abraão, T024-3361 5404, www. ilhagrandemanaca.com.br. Friendly French-Brazilian *pousada* right on the beach with homey light blue rooms decked out with colourful floor tiles, raw brick and with baclonies overlooking the little garden and the

beach. Public areas are decorated with art from the Amazon. Wi-Fi throughout.
$$ Ancoradouro, R da Praia 121, T024-3361 5153, www.pousad ancoradouro.com.br. Clean, simple rooms with en suite in a beach-front building, 10 mins' walk east of the jetty.
$$ Aqua Rio Hostel, Town Beach, Abraão, T024-3361 5405, www. aquariohostel.com. Party hostel on a peninsula overlooking the beach. Dorms, scruffy rooms, a large, relaxing bar area, seawater pool and great ocean views.
$$ Che Lagarto Ilha Grande Hostel, Town Beach, Abraão, T024-3361 9669, www.che lagarto.com. Large beachside party hostel with well-kept dorms, doubles, bar and tours including trail walking and kayaking.
$$ IYHA Albergue Holdandes, R Assembleia de Deus, T024-3361 5034, www.holandeshostel.com.br. Book ahead. Dorms, doubles and 4 little chalets in the forest on the edge of town. Breakfast included, laundry and advice on boats and tours. Good atmosphere.
$$ Porto Girassol, R do Praia 65, T011-3085 0289/021-99918 7255, http://ilhagrande.org/portogirassol. Simple whitewash a/c rooms with pine beds and bedside tables are in a mock-colonial beach house set in a small garden, 5 mins' east of the jetty. The best have balconies with ocean views.
$$ Pousada Bossa Nova, R Santana 145, T024-3361 5668, www.ilha grande.org/ bossanova. Cosy little *pousada* on the town's main street, with spacious rooms (the biggest can

accommodate 5 people) with arty beach beatnik driftwood-beds, big mirrors, plenty of raw wood and local art on the walls. A big TV lounge at the back opens onto a flower-filled garden.

$$ Pousada Cachoeira, 12-min walk from centre, T024-3361 9521, www. cachoeira.com. Price per person. Great little *pousada* full of character, with small rooms in chalets in a forest garden. Run by a German-Brazilian couple; English spoken. Good breakfast.

$$ Pousada Sanhaço, R Santana 120, T024-3361 5102, www.pousada sanhaco.com. A range of a/c rooms, the best of which have balconies with sea views and cosy en suites. The *pousada* is decorated with paintings by local artists. Wi-Fi throughout, generous breakfast.

$ Estalagem Costa Verde, R Amâncio Felicio de Souza 239a, half a block behind the church, T024-3361 5808, www.estalagemcostaverde.com. br. Bright hostel with light, well-maintained rooms decorated with a little thought. Great value.

Camping Camping Bicao, R Rua do Bicão s/n, T024-3361 5061, www. ilhagrande.org/campingdobicao. Hot showers, lockers, electricity a campsite with lots of shade. There are plenty of other campsites – see www. ilhagrande.com for details in English.

Paraty *p131, map p133*
There are many options in Paraty and 2 beautiful places in the hills nearby. **Hidden Pousadas Brazil**, www.hiddenpousadasbrazil.com, has some attractive options in the old town and around. **Ponta do Corumbe**, T024-9981 2610, www. pontadocorumbe.com.br, has the best of the *pousadas*, private houses and homestays in and around Paraty, including on the myriad beautiful beaches, islands and peninsulas in the bay. The most exclusive have private beaches, and the properties include the stunning Bernardes Jacobsen house used for the honey moon scene in Twilight Breaking Dawn. Also browse www.paraty.com. br/frame.htm.

$$$$ Bromelias Pousada and Spa, Rodovia Rio–Santos, Km 562, Graúna, T024-3371 2791, www. pousadabromelias.com.br. An Asian-inspired spa *pousada* with its own aromatherapy products and a range of massage treatments. Accommodation is in tastefully decorated chalets perched on a hillside forest garden overlooking the sea and islands.

$$$$ Pousada do Ouro, R Dr Pereira (or da Praia) 145, T024-3371 1311, www.pousadaouro.com.br. Near Paraty's eastern waterfront and built as a private home with a fortune made on the gold route. Plain rooms in an annexe and suites in the main building. The tropical garden houses an open-air poolside pavilion. Pictures of previous guests such as Mick Jagger, Tom Cruise and Linda Evangelista adorn the lobby.

$$$$ Pousada do Sandi, Largo do Rosário 1, T024-3371 2100, www.pousadadosandi.com.br. The most comfortable in town set in an 18th-century building with a grand lobby, comfortable mock-colonial rooms and a very good adjoining restaurant and pool area. Superior breakfast, parking and excellent tours organized through www.angatu.com.

$$$$ Pousada Pardieiro, R do Comércio 74, T024-3371 1370, www.pousadapardieiro.com.br. Tucked away in a quiet corner, with a calm, sophisticated atmosphere. Attractive colonial building with lovely gardens, delightful rooms facing internal patios and a little swimming pool. No children under 15.

$$$ Le Gite d'Indaitiba, Rodovia Rio–Santos (BR-101) Km 562, Graúna, T024-3371 7174, www.legitedindaiatiba.com.br. French-owned *pousada* with one of the best restaurants in southeastern Brazil. Sweeping views of the sea and bay of islands and a 2-m-wide spring water swimming pool.

$$$ Morro do Forte, R Orlando Carpinelli, T024-3371 1211, www.pousadamorroforte.com.br. Lovely garden, good breakfast, pool, German owner Peter Kallert offers trips on his yacht. Out of the centre. Recommended.

$$$ Pousada Bartholomeu, R Dr Samuel Costa 176, T024-3371 5032, www.bartholomeuparaty.com.br. A handsome Portuguese townhouse, with a handful of simple rooms in a situated above Alexandre Righetti's gourmet restaurant.

$$$ Vivenda and Maris, R Beija Flor 9 and Flor 11, Caboré, www.vivenda paraty.com and www.marisparaty.

com.br. These identical-twin *pousadas*, with lovely garden chalet rooms in bright white and marble clustered around a jewel-like pool, offer friendly, personal service and quiet, intimate and discreet accommodation 10 mins' walk from the city centre.

$$ Chill Inn Hostel and Pousada, R Orlando Carpinelli 3, Praia do Pontal, T024-3371 2545, www.chillinnhostel. com. Beachfront accommodation from dorms (**$** pp) to private rooms, all with bathrooms and a/c. Breakfast at beach bar, free taxi and internet.

$$ Geko Hostel, R Orlando Carpinelli 5, Praia do Pontal, T024-3371 7504, www.gekohostel.com. Doubles and dorms (**$** pp), breakfast included, free pickup from bus station, Wi-Fi, tours arranged.

$$ Pousada Arte Colonial, R da Matriz 292, T024-3371 7231, www.pousada artecolonial.com.br. One of the best deals in Paraty. A beautiful colonial building in the centre decorated with style and a personal touch by its French owner, with artefacts and antiques from all over the world.

$$ Pousada Capitão, R Luiz do Rosário 18, T024-3371 1815, www.paraty.com.br/capitao. Converted colonial building, close to the historic centre, swimming pool, English and Japanese spoken.

$$ Pousada do Corsário, Beco do Lapeiro 26, T024-3371 1866, www.pousadacorsario.com.br. With a pool and its own gardens, next to the river and 2 blocks from the centre. Simple, stylish rooms, most with hammocks outside. With a branch in Búzios (see website).

$$ Solar dos Gerânios, Praça da Matriz, T024-3371 1550, www. paraty.com.br/geranio. Beautiful colonial family house on the main square in traditional rustic style that is a welcome antidote to the more polished *pousadas*.

$ Casa do Rio, R Antônio Vidal 120, T024-3371 2223, www.paratyhostel. com. Youth hostel in a little house with riverside courtyard and hammocks. There's a kitchen and price includes breakfast. Trips by jeep or on horseback to waterfalls, mountains and beaches. Dorms a little crowded.

$ Pousada do Careca, Praça Macedo Soares, T024-3371 1291, ww.pousadadocareca.com. Simple rooms. Those without street windows are musty.

Camping
Camping Beira-Rio, just across the bridge, before the road to the fort.
Camping Clube do Brasil, Av Orlando Carpinelli, Praia do Pontal, T024-3371 1877. Small, good, very crowded in Jan and Feb, US$8 per person.

Trindade *p135*
Expect no frills in Trindade.
$ Chalé e Pousada Magia do Mar, T024-3371 5130. Thatched hut with space for 4. Views out over the beach.
$ Ponta da Trindade Pousada and Camping, T024-3371 5113. Simple fan-cooled rooms and a sand-floored campsite with cold showers and no electricity.
$ Pousada Marimbá, R Principal, T024-3371 5147. Simple colourful rooms and a breakfast area.

Around Trindade *p136*
$$ Ponta Negra homestays, Ponta Negra, contact **Teteco**, T024-3371 2673, teteco@paratyweb.com.br, or **Cauê**, francocvc@hotmail.com.

🍴 Restaurants

Ilha Grande *p129*
Aside from **Sito do Lobo** (guests only, see Where to stay, above), food on the island is fairly basic: fish, chicken or meat with beans, rice and chips. There are plenty of restaurants serving these exciting combinations in Abraão. We list the very few better options.
$$$ Lua e Mar, Abraão, on the waterfront, T024-3361 5113. The best seafood restaurant in Abraão with a menu including Bobó do Camarão, fish fillets and various moquecas.
$$ Dom Mario, R da Praia, T024-3361 5349. Good Franco-Brazilian dishes and seafood from a chef who honed his art at the Meridien in Rio. Try the fillet of fish in passion fruit sauce.

Paraty *p131, map p133*
The best restaurants in Paraty are in the historic part of town and are among the best in the southeast outside Rio or São Paulo. Watch out for surreptitious cover charges for live music, which are often very discreetly displayed. The less expensive restaurants, those offering *comida a quilo* (pay by weight) and the fast-food outlets are outside the historic centre, mainly on Av Roberto Silveira.

Paraty's regional specialities include *peixe à Parati* (local fish cooked with herbs and green bananas), served with *pirão* (a mixture of manioc flour and the sauce that the fish was cooked in). Also popular is the *filé de peixe ao molho de camarão* (fried fish fillet with a shrimp and tomato sauce). There is plenty of choice in Paraty so have a browse. Also see **Le Gite d'Indaitiba**, page 139.

$$$ Bartolomeu, R Samuel Costa 179, T024-3371 5032, www.bartholomeuparaty.com.br. A sumptuous menu of European-Brazilian fusion dishes (including a delicious, tangy bass (*robalo*) fillet with plantain purée (*puree de banana da terra*) and pumpkin sauce (*emoção de abóbora*). Be sure to try the guava petit gateau with cheese and walnut sorbet, which melts on the tongue, and kick off a meal with one of the tangerine and passion fruit caipirinhas.

$$$ Caminho do Ouro, R Samuel Costa 236, T024-3371 1689. Mineira Ronara Toledo cooks caiçara food with a gourmet twist using locally produced ingredients. Try her filet mignon in *jabuticaba* sauce or her bass in passion fruit and *pupunha* berry sauce.

$$$ Punto Di Vino, R Mcal Deodoro 129, historical centre, T024-3371 1348. The best for seafood in town; owned and run by a Neapolitan who catches his own 'catch of the day'. Great wood-fired pizza, live music and an excellent selection of wine.

$$$ Thai Brasil, R Dona Geralda 345, historic centre, T024-3371 0127, www.thaibrasil.com.br. Well-executed Thai standards without spices (Brazilians yelp in pain at the sight of a chilli).

$$ Vila Verde, Estr Paraty–Cunha, Km 7, T024-3371 7808, www.villaverde paraty.com.br. It's worth a stop off here on the way to or from the waterfalls, the Caminho Douro or Cunha. The restaurant serves light Italian and its open sides overlook a tropical garden that attracts numerous morpho butterflies, humming birds and tanagers.

$ Kontiki, Ilha Duas Irmãs, T024-9999 9599, www.ilhakontiki.com.br. Daily 1000-1500 and Fri and Sat for dinner. A tiny island, 5 mins from the pier where a small speed boat runs a (free) shuttle service. Wonderful island setting; ordinary food. Reservations recommended.

⊕ Entertainment

Paraty *p131, map p133*
Theatre
Teatro Espaço, R Dona Geralda 327, T024-3371 1575, www.ecparaty.org.br. Wed, Sat 2100, US$12. This world-famous puppet show should not be missed. The puppets tell stories (in mime), which are funny, sad, even shocking, with incredible realism. The short pieces (lasting 1 hr) are works of pure imagination and emotion and a moving commentary on the human condition.

⊕ Festivals

Paraty *p131, map p133*
Feb/Mar Carnaval, hundreds of people cover their bodies in black mud and run through the streets yelling like prehistoric creatures (anyone can join in).

Mar/Apr Semana Santa (Easter Week) with religious processions and folk songs.
Jul FLIP (Easter Week)
Mid-Jul Semana de Santa Rita, traditional foods, shows, exhibitions and dances.
Aug Festival da Pinga, the *cachaça* fair at which local distilleries display their products and there are plenty of opportunities to over-indulge.
Sep (around the 8th) **Semana da Nossa Senhora dos Remédios**, processions and religious events.
Sep/Oct Spring Festival of Music, concerts in front of Santa Rita Church.
31 Dec New Year's Eve, a huge party with open-air concerts and fireworks (reserve accommodation in advance).

☉ What to do

Angra dos Reis and around *p128*
See **Angatu**, under Paraty, below.

Ilha Grande *p129*
Boat trips
These are easy to organize on the quay in Abraão on Ilha Grande.

Scuba diving
Ilha Grande Dive, R da Praia s/n, Vila do Abraão, T021-3361 5512, igdive@bol.com.br (next to the *farmacia* on the seafront). Offers trips around the entire bay.

Paraty *p131, map p133*
Angatu, T011-3872 0945, www. angatu.com. The best private tours and diving around the bay in luxurious yachts and motor cruisers, with private entries to the exclusive island parties. Also offers private villa rental in and around Paraty (see Where to stay, page 138). Book well ahead. Highly recommended.
Antígona, Praça da Bandeira 2, Centro Histórico, T024-3371 1165, www.antigona.com.br. Daily schooner tours, 5 hrs, bar and lunch on board. Recommended.
Paraty Tours, Av Roberto Silveira 11, T024-3371 1327, www.paratytours. com.br. Good range of trips. English and Spanish spoken.
Rei Cigano, contact through **Bartolomeu** restaurant (see Restaurants, page 141), or ring Tuca T024-7835 3190, thiparaty@hotmail. com. Day excursions and overnights or even expeditions along the Brazilian coast in a beautiful 60-ft sailing schooner with cabins.
Soberana da Costa, R Dona Geraldo 43, in **Pousada Mercado do Pouso**, T024-3371 1114. Schooner trips. Recommended.

⊖ Transport

Angra dos Reis and around *p128*
Bus Costa Verde buses run at least hourly to the *rodoviária* in **Rio de Janeiro**, some are direct, others take the *via litoral* and go through Barra, Ipanema and Copacabana, US$10, 2½ hrs. Sit on the right for the best views. Busy at weekends. There are also regular buses to and from **São Paulo**, **Paraty**, **Ubatuba** and the São Paulo coast.

Ferry Ferries run to Ilha Grande, see below. Fishing boats will also take passengers for around US$5 per person before 1300 or when full. Boat charter costs around US$60-100.

Ilha Grande *p129*

For the most up to date boat and ferry timetables see www.ilhagrande.org. **Ferry** Fishing boats and ferries (**Barcas SA**, T021-2533 7524) leave from Angra dos Reis, Conceição de Jacareí and Mangaratiba, taking 2 hrs or so to reach **Vila do Abraão**, the island's only real village. From Angra there are 4 daily yachts and catamarans and one ferry (at 1000) leaving 0730-1600, and an extra ferry at 1330 on weekends and public holidays. From Conceição de Jacareí there are 7 yacht sailings daily 0900-1815, with an occasional late boat at 2100 on busy Fri. From Mangaratiba there is a ferry at 0800 and a yacht at 1400. Schedules change frequently and it's well worth checking www. ilhagrande.org, which details the names and phone numbers of all boats currently sailing. Ferries cost US$4 on weekdays and double that on weekends, yachts US$8 and catamarans US$30. Buy at least 1 hr in advance to ensure this price, and a place. Note the Angra catamaran leaves from Santa Luiza pier (not the ferry pier). All the towns are served by Costa Verde buses leaving from the *rodoviária* in Rio. **Easy Transfer**, T021-7753 2190, www.easytransfer brazil.com, offers a van and boat service from Rio to Ilha Grande; door to door from the city (US$37) and from the airport (price depends on flight times and numbers); and from Ilha Grande to Paraty (US$25). There are discounts on multi-trips (eg Rio–Ilha Grande–Paraty–Rio).

Paraty *p131, map p133*

Bus On public holidays and in high season, the frequency of bus services usually increases. **Costa Verde** runs 9 buses a day to **Rio de Janeiro** (241 km, 4 hrs, US$10). To **Angra dos Reis** (98 km, 1½ hrs, every 1 hr 40 mins, US$5); 3 a day to **Ubatuba** (75 km, just over 1 hr, São José company, US$5), **Taubaté** (170 km) and **Guaratinguetá** (210 km); 2 a day to **São Paulo**, 1100 and 2335 (304 km via **São José dos Campos**, 5½ hrs, US$12 (**Reunidas** book up quickly and are very busy at weekends), and **São Sebastião**. **Easy Transfer** (see Ilha Grande, above) offers transfers along the Costa Verde to and from Paraty. To **Ilha Grande** costs US$25 and to **Rio** US$40.

Taxi Set rate of US$5 for trips within the historic centre.

Trindade and around *p135*

Paraty–Ubatuba buses all pass the turning to Trindade and will pick you up from here. In high season there are vans from Trindade to the turning (US$5). There are 14 direct **Colitur** (T024-3371 1224, www.paraty trindade.com.br) buses a day running between Paraty and Trindade which also call in on **Laranjeiras** for the trailhead to **Sono** and **Ponta Negra**.

🕒 Directory

Ilha Grande *p129*
Banks Only open at weekends.

Paraty *p131, map p133*
Banks **Banco do Brasil**, Av Roberto Silveira, just outside the historic centre, ATM. Exchange 1100-1430, ask for the manager.

Contents

Footnotes

Basic Portuguese for travellers

Learning Portuguese is a useful part of the preparation for a trip to Brazil and no volume of dictionaries, phrase books or word lists will provide the same enjoyment as being able to communicate directly with the people of the country you are visiting. It is a good idea to make an effort to grasp the basics before you go. As you travel you will pick up more of the language and the more you know, the more you will benefit from your stay.

General pronunciation

Within Brazil itself, there are variations in pronunciation, intonation, phraseology and slang. This makes for great richness and for the possibility of great enjoyment in the language. A couple of points which the newcomer to the language will spot immediately are the use of the tilde (~) over 'a' and 'o'. This makes the vowel nasal, as does a word ending in 'm' or 'ns', or a vowel followed by 'm' + consonant, or by 'n' + consonant. Another important point of spelling is that for words ending in 'i' and 'u' the emphasis is on the last syllable, though (unlike Spanish) no accent is used. This is especially relevant in place names like Buriti, Guarapari, Caxambu, Iguaçu. Note also the use of 'ç', which changes the pronunciation of c from hard [k] to soft [s].

Personal pronouns

In conversation, most people refer to 'you' as *você*, although in the south and in Pará *tu* is more common. To be more polite, use *O Senhor/A Senhora*. For 'us', *gente* (people, folks) is very common when it includes you too.

Portuguese words and phrases

Greetings and courtesies

hello	*oi*	thank you	*obrigado* (if a man is speaking)/
good morning	*bom dia*		*obrigada* (if a
good afternoon	*boa tarde*		woman is speaking)
good evening/night	*boa noite*		
goodbye	*adeus/tchau*	thank you	*muito obrigado/*
see you later	*até logo*	very much	*muito obrigada*
please	*por favor/*	how are you?	*como vai você tudo*
	faz favor		*bem?/tudo bom?*
		I am fine	*vou bem/tudo bem*

pleased to meet you	*um prazer*	please speak slowly	*fale devagar*
no	*não*		*por favor*
yes	*sim*	what is your name?	*qual é seu nome?*
excuse me	*com licença*	my name is …	*o meu nome é …*
I don't understand	*não entendo*	go away!	*vai embora!*

Basic questions

where is?	*onde está/*	when?	*quando?*
	onde fica?	I want to go to …	*quero ir para …*
why?	*por que?*	when does the bus	*a que hor sai/*
how much does	*quanto*	leave?/arrive?	*chega o ônibus?*
it cost?	*custa?*	is this the way to	*aquí é o caminho*
what for?	*para que?*	the church?	*para a igreja?*
how much is it?	*quanto é?*		
how do I get to … ?	*para chegar*		
	a … ?		

Basics

bathroom/toilet	*banheiro*	exchange rate	*a taxa de câmbio*
police (policeman)	*a polícia*	notes/coins	*notas/moedas*
	(o polícia)	cash	*dinheiro*
hotel	*o (a pensão,*	breakfast	*o caféde manh*
	a hospedaria)	lunch	*o almoço*
restaurant	*o restaurante*	dinner/supper	*o jantar*
	(o lanchonete)	meal	*a refeição*
post office	*o correio*	drink	*a bebida*
telephone office	*(central)*	mineral water	*a água mineral*
	telefônica	soft fizzy drink	*o refrigerante*
supermarket	*o supermercado*	beer	*a cerveja*
market	*o mercado*	without sugar	*sem açúcar*
bank	*o banco*	without meat	*sem carne*
bureau de change	*a casa de*		
	câmbio		

Getting around

on the left/right	*à esquerda/*	train	*a trem*
	à direita	airport	*o aeroport*
straight on	*direto*	aeroplane/airplane	*o avião*
to walk	*caminhar*	flight	*o vôa*
bus station	*a rodoviária*	first/second class	*primeira/*
bus	*o ônibus*		*segunda clase*
bus stop	*a parada*	train station	*a ferroviária*

| combined bus and train station | a rodoferroviária | ticket | o passagem/ o bilhete |
| | | ticket office | a bilheteria |

Accommodation

room	quarto	hot/cold water	água quente/fria
noisy	barulhento	to make up/clean	limpar
single/double room	(quarto de) solteiro/(quarto para) casal	sheet(s)	o lençol (os lençóis)
		blankets	as mantas
room with two beds	quarto com duas camas	pillow	o travesseiro
		clean/dirty towels	as toalhas limpas/sujas
with private bathroom	quarto com banheiro	toilet paper	o papel higiêico

Health

chemist	a farmacia	condoms	as camisinhas/ os preservativos
doctor	o coutor/ a doutora	contraceptive (pill)	anticonceptional (a pílula)
(for) pain	(para) dor		
stomach	o esômago (a barriga)	period	a menstruação/ a regra
head	a cabeça	sanitary towels/	toalhas absorventes/
fever/sweat	a febre/o suor higiênicas	tampons	absorventes internos
diarrhoea	a diarréia	contact lenses	lentes de contacto
blood	o sangue		

Time

at one o'clock (am/pm)	a uma hota (da manhã/ da tarde)	it's seven o'clock	são sete horas
		it's twenty past six/ six twenty	são seis e vinte
at half past two/ two thirty	as dois e meia	it's five to nine	são cinco para as nove
at a quarter to three	quinze para as três	in ten minutes	em dez minutos
		five hours	cinco horas
it's one o'clock	é uma	does it take long?	sura muito?

Days

Monday	*segunda feiro*	Friday	*sexta feira*
Tuesday	*terça feira*	Saturday	*sábado*
Wednesday	*quarta feira*	Sunday	*domingo*
Thursday	*quinta feira*		

Months

January	*janeiro*	July	*julho*
February	*fevereiro*	August	*agosto*
March	*março*	September	*setembro*
April	*abril*	October	*outubro*
May	*maio*	November	*novembro*
June	*junho*	December	*dezembro*

Numbers

one	*um/uma*	fifteen	*quinze*
two	*dois/duas*	sixteen	*dezesseis*
three	*três*	seventeen	*dezessete*
four	*quatro*	eighteen	*dezoito*
five	*cinco*	nineteen	*dezenove*
six	*seis* ('meia' half, is frequently used for number 6 ie half-dozen)	twenty	*vinte*
		twenty-one	*vente e um*
		thirty	*trinta*
		forty	*cuarenta*
seven	*sete*	fifty	*cinqüe*
eight	*oito*	sixty	*sessenta*
nine	*nove*	seventy	*setenta*
ten	*dez*	eighty	*oitenta*
eleven	*onze*	ninety	*noventa*
twelve	*doze*	hundred	*cem, cento*
thirteen	*treze*	thousand	*mil*
fourteen	*catorze*		

Useful slang

that's great/cool	*que legal*	cheesy/tacky	*brega*
bloke/guy/geezer	*cara* (literally 'face')	posh, spoilt girl/boy with rich parents	*patricinha/*
biker slang for bloke/guy	*mano*		*mauricinho*
		in fashion/cool	*descolado*

Index

Titles available in the Footprint *Focus* range

For the latest books, e-books and a wealth of travel information, visit us at: www.footprinttravelguides.com.

footprinttravelguides.com

Join us on facebook for the latest travel news, product releases, offers and amazing competitions: www.facebook.com/footprintbooks.